THE MUSIC
OF MARRIAGE

TO HAVE SWEET MUSIC IN OUR
HOMES, WE NEED MELODY,
HARMONY, AND RHYTHM

ADRIAN ROGERS

innovo
PUBLISHING
innovopublishing.com

Published by Innovo Publishing, LLC
www.innovopublishing.com
1-888-546-2111

Providing Full-Service Publishing Services for Christian Authors, Artists &
Ministries: Books, eBooks, Audiobooks, Music, Screenplays, Film & Curricula

THE MUSIC OF MARRIAGE

ISBN: 978-1-61314-793-1

Cover Design: Jeff Hatcher
Interior Layout: Innovo Publishing, LLC

Printed in the United States of America
U.S. Printing History
First Edition: 2021

Has God called you to create a Christian book, eBook, audiobook, music album,
screenplay, film, or curricula? If so, visit the ChristianPublishingPortal.com to
learn how to accomplish your calling with excellence. Learn to do everything
yourself, or hire trusted Christian Experts from our Marketplace to help.

CONTENTS

"God created us differently so that He might make us one. We aren't just created to sing in unity; we were also made to make beautiful music through harmony."

—*Adrian Rogers*

Chapter One

HARMONY IN THE HOME

At one point, I had been thinking a lot about music. I decided it was time for me to sing a solo in church. I went to talk to our music minister about this.

I said, "Brother Jim, may I sing in church?"

He said, "Yes, pastor. You are the pastor. If you want to sing in church, you may."

I then asked, "What song would you like me to sing?"

He answered, with a grin, "How about...*On a Hill Far Away?*"

In all seriousness, I don't know a whole lot about music. However, there are a few things that I do know. For example, I know that music is made up of three parts: melody, harmony, and rhythm. To achieve melody, you need to sing the same song. This is what husbands and wives need to do.

To achieve harmony, you sing different parts that sound good together. A husband and wife may sing the same song, but they don't sing the same parts. To achieve rhythm, spouses must sing together at the same tempo. To have sweet music in our homes, we need melody, harmony, and rhythm.

Let's look at what the Bible has to say about the music in the home. Consider the words of Genesis 1:27, and let's look at God's grand design.

THE MUSIC OF MARRIAGE

God's Divine Design

"So God created man in His own image; in the image of God He created him; male and female He created them" (Genesis 1:27). Male and female. God thought up the idea of boys and girls. We didn't think it up. The unisex idea was not created by God; it was born in Hell.

God made men and women, male and female. God did that by divine design. Both the man and the woman are made in the image of God. A woman is absolutely as valuable and as important, as gifted, and all of the other things, as any man could possibly be. Truly, the Bible teaches that God does not value one sex above another.

According to Paul in Galatians 3:28, "There is neither Jew nor Greek, there is neither slave nor free, there is neither male nor female; for you are all one in Christ Jesus." Now he's not talking about society. He's not saying that there's to be a blurring of the distinction between the sexes, but he is saying in Christ, male and female, bond and free, we're all one. We're all valuable.

Despite that, God has made us different. God made us different that He might make us one. And I thank God for the difference. I want us to celebrate today because it's our differences, not our likenesses, which bring us together as husbands and wives. How important is it that we be brought together as husbands and wives? The Bible says in Ecclesiastes 4:9, "Two are better than one…." And that is so true.

Let's talk about that divine design. God created this design, the difference in the sexes. And He did this for a purpose. What is that purpose? As we look at Genesis 2:18, we read, "And the LORD God said, it is not good that the man should be alone; I will make him a helper comparable to him."

This particular verse is toward the end of the creation. God considers everything that He has made. And he says, "It's good!"

Everything God created He would say, "That's good, that's good, and that's good."

Then, God created man, and He said, "That's not good. Man does not need to be alone. I'll send someone to help him."

At this moment in history, that's where the divine design began. God knew that man did not need to be alone. He needed help. So, God created the woman. This is where God's perfect composition started. The beautiful music of the home began in the Garden of Eden.

Three Reasons for God to Create Males And Females

As we contemplate God's divine design for the home, there are three reasons God created both males and females.

First, God created males and females for companionship. It is not good that man should be alone. None of the animals could satisfy the hunger in Adam's heart. Not even God Himself could meet the desires of man's heart for companionship.

Think about it. It's incredible. Adam had a face-to-face relationship with Almighty God in the Garden of Eden, and yet that could not satisfy the deepest need that Adam had. He had a longing for something more. So, God created the woman. In my own life, I thank God for the precious companion that He's given me in Joyce.

A second reason God created males and females was for cooperation. Notice what the verse says about the design, "I will make a helper" for him. Some translations use the word *"helpmeet."* Now the word "helper" in this verse is a noun; it is not a verb. God is not saying that He is going to give Adam some help. God could have given Adam a friend to help him pick fruit, a buddy, or somebody. No that's not the idea.

The idea of *"helpmeet"* is someone who is going to cooperate with Adam. Someone who will become a part of a team with him. Someone who will make him more than he could have been without that particular person. Someone to help Adam to reach his full potential.

Indeed, Adam could not have been what he ought to have been, in my estimation, at all, without Eve. In my life, I could not be what I ought to be without Joyce. I'm blessed because Joyce has been this helper to me throughout my life, our married life, and our ministry.

When Joyce and I dated in high school, I was playing football and she was a cheerleader. One of the pictures that hangs on the wall of our home is a picture of her in her cheerleading outfit. Inscribed in the frame of that photo are the words, "To Adrian, I will always cheer you on."

This has been true for our entire marriage. Even as I left the home to go preach recently, Joyce threw her arms around me and kissed me. Then, she said, "There goes my preacher and my mighty warrior." She sent me out to preach with a kiss, a hug, and great words of encouragement. (I preach better because of the kiss!) God created women for companionship and cooperation. **Additionally, God created the woman to be a completion to the man.** In Genesis 2:18, God says, "I will make a helpmeet for him" (KJV). To be a helpmeet is to be a fitting helper, someone to make up that part which is lacking. To be a helpmeet is to be the other half. Some will say, "the better half."

Indeed, it is not mere folklore that God took Eve from Adam's side. It is that something is missing until she is returned. And it is not by mere happenstance one speaks of the husband or wife as "the other half." We are half-people without our mates. That's the way God designed it. It is His divine design.

In musical terms, you might think of Adam as a violin; you think of Eve as the bow. And it is together that they make the music that they are supposed to make. She is to complete Adam. She is to make him better than he would have been on his own.

Also, women were created to be the completer, not the competitor. Women are to complete their husbands, not to finish them off. It's not meant to be a battle or a competition. God's idea was for us to come together and make each other better, stronger, and more dynamic than we would have ever been as singles.

Celebrating the Definite Differences between Men and Women

Because of God's divine design, He made a difference in the sexes. In Genesis 1:27, we read, "Male and female He created them."

It's true. Men and women are different. And we don't need the Bible to tell us that. Our differences are not just physiological, they are also deeply emotional and spiritual. Psychologists tell us these things.

For a long time, radical feminists have been trying to tell us that all of the differences, the emotional differences, and the psychological differences are only cultural. They are not only cultural. They are creational. And there's a difference, for example, in the way that the brains of men and women are wired.

Researchers tell us that boys have a predominant proclivity in the right side of the brain and for girls it's the left side. For this reason, boys tend to be a little more physical and women tend to be more verbal. For the most part, little girls will begin to talk quicker than little boys. Have you noticed these things?

Psychologists, like Dr. James Dobson[1] and others, have written much on the differences between boys and girls. For example, if you send a little boy off to a birthday party, what will he do? He'll rip and tear and pull the girls' hair and smear the cake and so forth. Little girls want to play the games like they are supposed to be played. That's because boys, by nature, are more aggressive.

Give the little girls a jigsaw puzzle and they try to put it together. You give it to a boy, and he may sling it across the room. Typically, when you give a little girl a doll, she wants to caress that doll, she wants to cuddle that doll. You give a little boy a doll, he'll make a hammer out of it. That's just the way he is. Boys and girls are different. God created them that way.

---

1. Waresak, JT. "Something My 7-Year-Old Knows that the Main Media Doesn't Regarding Boys and Girls." *Family Talk*, 29 July 2021, drjamesdobson.org/blogs/jt-waresak/something-my-7-year-old-knows-main-media-doesnt-regarding-boys-and-girls.

Many today are trying to change these natural proclivities. However, they are built in by God. They are part of the way God designed us.

Consider high school students. Go to a high school and watch the way boys carry books and girls carry books. Typically, boys will put their books under the arm and carry them to the side. But, how do the girls usually carry their books? Cradled up in their arms, like the books are valuable. Nothing is wrong with either of the ways of carrying books. My point is this: there is a divine design and a definite difference.

These differences are not cultural; they are created. Why? Because of what God made the man and the woman to do.

One difference we find in these passages is that **God made the man to be a provider and God made the woman to be the helper**, a helpmeet for him. In Genesis 2:15, we read, "Then the LORD God took the man and put him in the Garden of Eden to tend and keep it." God said to the man, "That's your job."

God said, "Adam, you're going to till the soil by the sweat of your face. Then, you are going to eat your bread." (See Genesis 3:19.) God designed for man to be the provider of the home. The woman was created to help the man to do what God created him to do. She is there as a help and support.

I realize that all of this may not seem politically correct or culturally savvy in today's society. However, this was God's original design. He purposefully and thoughtfully organized things to work well in this way. When men and women live by God's design, things go so much better.

Of course, there are seasons and reasons that a man cannot provide. Perhaps because of illness or injury, a wife must step in and be the provider. Whenever possible, however, I believe that a man should work and provide for his family. God created men to bear this burden and shoulder this responsibility.

If it is a two-income family, and the woman perhaps works out of the home or has a side job, it's hopeful that she can still enjoy as much time as possible with her children. In my opinion, the husband's income should be used for food, shelter, clothing, and transportation. And the woman's income, if possible now, should be that supplementary income, but not the main support. If not, there can be bitterness and division and the wife can become tough-minded in a way that God did not intend for her to become.

A second difference we find in God's design is that the man is to be the protector while the woman is to be the nurturer. God made man to protect the woman. Think about it. When Eve sinned, God blamed Adam. Did you know that?

In Genesis 3:17, we read, "Then to Adam He said, 'Because you have heeded the voice of your wife, and have eaten from the tree of which I commanded you, saying, "You shall not eat of it": cursed is the ground for your sake; in toil you shall eat of it all the days of your life.'"

God cursed the ground for Adam's sake, not Eve's. Adam was to blame. Romans 5:12 backs up this idea. When the Bible says that sin came into the world, it doesn't blame Eve, it blames Adam. In Romans 5:12, we read, "Therefore, just as through one man sin entered the world, and death through sin, and thus death spread to all men...."

It's a Bible truth: the husband is meant to protect his wife. Moreover, a wife needs a husband who will protect her. And children need fathers who are protectors.

We need husbands and fathers who will set limits for children, not dropout dads, but dads who will say "no" to boys and to girls. It is essential in our day for our men to step up and protect their families as they never have before. Men need to take responsibility and lead well.

Thirdly, God made men to be the leaders and women to be the enhancers. For example, in Genesis 3:16, God said to the wife, "Your desire shall be for your husband, and he shall rule over you." The husband is the leader. But the woman is the enhancer.

An example of this difference is found in Genesis 3:20, "And Adam called his wife's name Eve, because she was the mother of all living." God made Adam to protect. God made Eve to enhance and look after all living things. He is to be a father.

She is to be a mother. Women just naturally add to, beautify, and upgrade their surroundings. God made women to be this way.

Consider the way men and women shop. Often, when men go shopping, they want to go to Lowe's or to the hardware store. Women, instead, would rather visit Hobby Lobby or a home furnishings store. Typically, men like to fix and mend things while women like to make things more comfortable and beautiful. These are God-given instincts—for both sexes.

Most men are content if they have food, shelter, a nice recliner, and a good TV with a remote. Women, on the other hand, like to be surrounded by beauty and by beautiful things. If men could understand this difference about their wives, they could live much happier lives!

A Few Differences That Are More Tendencies

Let's talk about a few things that are the tendencies of men and women. These are not hard and fast rules. These are general considerations about males and females.

For example, as a tendency, the man is stronger than the woman. That's just one of the tendencies. The man is physically strong. Now not always. I mean some women can beat up some men. And, I don't want to mess with these women! But as a rule, if we put all the men on one side of the room and all the women on the other side and had a fight, more men would win based on brute strength.

Additionally, the Bible says in 1 Peter 3:7, that the woman is the "weaker vessel." Why? Because of what God created men and women to do. What were men created to do? Tend the Garden. Man has to be able to dig and to chop and to carry and to protect and to provide. What did God make the woman to do? She is the mother of all of the living, she is to be gentle. She is to be tender, she is to nurture and to take care of everyone and everything.

Have you ever watched a woman as she'll see a little kitten, how she'll be with a kitten? I mean she just wants to be tender. That's just her nature.

On the other hand, have you ever watched a man change a diaper? Whoomp! I mean, it's like you're putting a saddle on a horse or something here. Most men just don't have that gentleness within them. Of course, they can learn to be kind and learn to change diapers. Yet, most commonly, gentleness is associated with females.

In my opinion, which may not be the popular view, I think it is the epitome of absurdity to try to put women in combat. Because of the way God designed men and women, men are much more fitted for the horrors and the challenges of war.

In 1948, Israel tried to press its women into combat. They needed soldiers so badly that they put the women into service in the battle lines. Do you know how long they kept them there? Three weeks. And they found out it was a tragic mistake. There was a loss of more lives on both sides. On the Israeli side, the men soldiers were fighting, not to win the battle, but to protect the women. They were risking their own lives to protect the women.

In that battle, more Israeli men lost their lives protecting the women. And on the other side, there were more Arab lives lost, because the Arabs were not going to allow themselves to be defeated by an army of women. They were throwing themselves in the battle. After three weeks, the Israeli military backed off and said, "We'll use the women behind the lines. Yes, we'll use them for support, but not in battle."

Quite frankly, I believe it's the one thing that keeps women from playing professional football. Women were not created to take the punishment of being hit and tackled over and over. Dear friend, God just made males and females different.

Another tendency of men is to approach problems head first. Women, as a rule, approach problems heart first. That's just the way they are. For the most part, women freely allow their emotions to come to the surface while men keep their emotions more submerged.

When you get into the male and female battle, the battle of the sexes, it's generally, not always, logic versus emotion. When I share this, some women get angry. You may think I don't know what I'm talking about. However, I don't mean this as a negative. It is amazing how God created women.

One thing that always astounds me is a woman's intuition. Women are typically so aware of what is going on around them, so observant, and so in tune with people and situations. Often, men will not be remotely aware of all that is happening around them.

I once heard a preacher teach that men are more like bulls and women are more like butterflies. When a breeze blows, the bull barely notices, but the butterfly feels it, senses the breeze, and is moved by it. Women have a sixth sense about them that men just don't have.

For example, I think about my wife. She is a scholar and made top grades in school. I would hate for you to see her report card and my report card. She was a much better student than I was. However, I'm not just talking about her intelligence, I'm also talking about the way she comes to a problem. I come to a problem head first, she comes to a problem heart first. By tendency, most women face problems differently than their male counterparts.

Another difference that often shows up is the way men and women face life. **As a rule, men are more success oriented while women are more security oriented.** Men are headed toward a certain goal and don't care who gets hurt. Women, on the other hand, take time to consider their options and the feelings of those around them. Women tend to make more well-thought-out decisions without rushing ahead too quickly.

Who's right, who's wrong? Neither is right or wrong, it's just simply the way that people come to the deal.

For example, a man will set a goal and then just go for it. He'll take the family savings and invest in a project, sometimes without consulting his wife. Many men will rush ahead and make decisions—allowing the consequences to be what they may.

When the typical woman wants to set a goal and accomplish something, she will often consult her husband, count the cost, make the plans, and then proceed. Women like to get things right, create beauty, and make things better for their husbands and families. For this reason, you don't often see women rush ahead without planning and forethought.

Another general rule of thought is that men are most concerned about their work and women are more concerned about their relationships. For a man, his work is an extension of himself. And if a man's work is not going right, he's not happy.

But for the most part, a woman sees her home, her family, and her relationships as an extension of herself. Of course, if she works, she cares deeply about her job. However, a woman will care much more about the state of the home and the children than the man. If a woman's home is cluttered, her life is cluttered. If her kids are struggling, she struggles too.

Most women are not primarily interested in success, but in feeling safe and secure. For you men, if you want your wife to be happy, don't just go out and buy her a big present and bring it home. You must also fix little things around the house, and care about how the children are doing.

My wife gets happy when, once every seven years, I'll get out a screwdriver and I'll fix something around the house. Why is that? Because when you fix those little things, you are letting your wife know that what matters to her matters to you also. Why not ask her for a "honey-do" list of little things you can do around the house to help with the home and the children?

In like manner, another difference between men and women is that men tend to look at the big picture. While, on the other hand, women often tend to look at the details. Being goal-oriented, a man will say, "In 4 to 5 years I'm going to do this thing."

Many women will want to know what is going to happen *between* now and the next 4 to 5 years. A man will announce his big plans to the woman without letting her know that he has thought about what is going to happen in between.

For me, I don't even think about what's going to happen in between. I'll look ahead, see a goal, and believe that by God's grace we can get there. I'll worry about the problems when I meet them.

These differences can cause real problems in our homes. For example, a man may come home from work one day and announce that he has discovered a great new product that can make a lot of money. He tells his wife that he has sold the house and wants to move the family to Cincinnati next month. Instantly, she begins to cry. He asks, "What's the matter? This is the best deal we've ever had. Can't you think straight?"

The woman is no longer crying. Now she is angry. He is angry. It becomes a huge mess! Why? Because she starts thinking of all of the details and says to him, "Don't you realize the kids are in braces and our dentist is right here? And do you realize it is four weeks to graduation? And what about our church and our friends? I don't want to leave this neighborhood."

The man has never thought about any of these details. He was just thinking about making money and a great job prospect. Because of the way he handled things, his wife becomes an adversary, rather than a companion. Rather than a completer, she becomes a competitor because he has not taken time to recognize her concerns and consult her before making this decision.

If he will take the time to discuss the move, the changes, and all of the details, this man can build back the relationship. They can be on the same team, but not without working together and appreciating each other's differences.

Also, a difference between men and women is that men tend to be insensitive, and women tend to be sensitive. Why is that? God made men with thicker skin, for the most part. If they were created to be out there on the work-front earning the living, they must be tough. The world is a difficult place, full of competition, danger and disagreeable things. If the man was created to be the protector and the provider, he must have some strength and resolve.

On the flip slide, in God's economy, women were created to nurture, take care of the home, and help their husbands. A woman's sensitivity is a gift and can greatly enhance a marriage and a family. Sensitivity is not a weakness; it is intense intuition and awareness.

A final difference between women and men, which is worth noting, is that men tend to be suspicious while women are more trusting. Because most men are highly protective, they are always on the lookout for danger. Often, I find myself just protecting my wife and my daughters and my grandchildren and just having a protective nature.

Often, women are more trusting. They trust their children. They believe the little darlings are always telling the truth. They trust their husbands. When nobody else believes in him, she believes in him. They are just that way.

A while back, we were in the Charlotte airport. It was during one of the wars in the Middle East. During this time, a lot of people were afraid to fly on airplanes because of terrorism. Over and over again in the airport, the announcement was made, "Do not take your eyes off your baggage; do not take gifts from someone else. Do not carry anyone else's baggage. Never leave your baggage unattended. Report any unattended baggage."

Joyce and I are waiting to board our flight, sitting and reading in the boarding area. Joyce looks over at me and says, "Adrian, there's something strange. I'm watching a young man's things for him, and he's been gone for a long time."

I looked at her and said, "You what?"

She said, "Yes. He came up to me and asked me to watch his bag for him."

I asked, "Who is he?"

Joyce answered, "I don't know."

I asked, "Where did he go?"

Again, she answered, "I don't know."

Then, I asked, "When will he be back?"

She answered, "He didn't say."

I then asked, "Which bag is it?

She said, "That one over there."

I looked at her and said, "Joyce, how could you do this? Didn't you hear all of those announcements?"

She answered, "Yes. But he was such a nice-looking young man. And, he had on a tie. You know terrorists never wear ties. He was so nice."

I immediately went to the airline counter and said, "Let me tell you what's happened. A young man left a bag with my wife. He's been gone for 15-20 minutes. I don't know who he is, where he's gone, or what is in the bag."

The gate agent looked at me and said, "That's a no-no."

I said, "It's her fault." (Not my finest moment.)

The airline immediately brought out security and took the bag away. On that day, I wasn't a very good protector. And, I realized how trusting my wife was of strangers. While I would have been suspicious, my Joyce was trusting. Why? Because that's the way God made her to be, to be receiving and trusting.

A Few Final Thoughts

Why did God make us so different? Why create men and women to be so unlike each other? God created us differently so that He might make us one. We aren't just created to sing in unity; we were also made to make beautiful music through harmony.

When Joyce lives in the beautiful way that God created her to live and I do too, we make amazing music. We need each other, we complement each other, and together the music of our marriage is sweet. That's the way God designed it to be.

Dear friends, the home is not a duet, it's a trio: a man, a woman, and Jesus Christ.

A Prayer for Our Homes

Father God, I pray in the name of Jesus that You would give us godly, Christian homes. Thank You, Lord, that You made us different, that You might make us one. In Jesus' Name, Amen.

"Dating and courtship should not end with the marriage ceremony. You need to turn up the heat and keep pursuing your wife."

—*Adrian Rogers*

Chapter Two

MELODY IN THE HOME

In the last chapter, we discussed the differences between men and women and the plan for us to make beautiful harmonious music. Our differences can make us one in Christ. Let's look next at the way God also desires for us to have melodies playing in our homes.

Look at Ephesians 5:17-33, a passage I like to call, *"The Music Chapter."*

> Therefore do not be unwise, but understand what the will of the Lord is. And do not be drunk with wine, in which is dissipation; but be filled with the Spirit, speaking to one another in psalms and hymns and spiritual songs, singing and making melody in your heart to the Lord, giving thanks always for all things to God the Father in the name of our Lord Jesus Christ, submitting to one another in the fear of God. Wives, submit to your own husbands, as to the Lord. For the husband is head of the wife, as also Christ is head of the church; and He is the Savior of the body. Therefore, just as the church is subject to Christ, so let the wives be to their own husbands in everything. Husbands, love your wives, just as Christ also loved the church and gave

Himself for her, that He might sanctify and cleanse her with the washing of water by the word, that He might present her to Himself a glorious church, not having spot or wrinkle or any such thing, but that she should be holy and without blemish. So husbands ought to love their own wives as their own bodies; he who loves his wife loves himself. For no one ever hated his own flesh, but nourishes and cherishes it, just as the Lord does the church. For we are members of His body, of His flesh and of His bones. "For this reason a man shall leave his father and mother and be joined to his wife, and the two shall become one flesh." This is a great mystery, but I speak concerning Christ and the church. Nevertheless let each one of you in particular so love his own wife as himself, and let the wife see that she respects her husband.

Let's think about music in our homes. For there to be music, and music that we like to listen to, there must be melody. We must sing the same song. There can be harmony; we sing different parts. There ought to be rhythm, where we sing it together in sync.

In the first chapter, we discussed many of the differences that make us one. Indeed, God made men and women different that he might make us one. How do we sing the same song? The man must sing one part and take the lead. Then, the woman will sing another part that harmonizes with her husband. That's simply God's plan.

Also, I shared with you a little bit about the differences between men and women. These psychological and physiological and emotional differences vary in degrees, but these are tendencies. What I have shared is not necessarily ironclad with every man and every woman. But we talked about God's divine design, how God made males and females.

Let me review those differences here:

- God teaches that the man is to be the provider and the woman is to be his helper.

- The man is to be a protector. The woman is to be a nurturer, she's the one who gives life.
- The man is the leader, and the woman is there to give beauty and enhancement to the home.
- Men are more physically strong; women are tenderer and more fragile.
- Men approach problems head first and women heart first.
- The man is the head of the home; the woman is the heart.
- Men, because it is their duty to provide, generally are more success oriented. Women generally are more security oriented.
- Men tend to look at the big picture to be goal oriented. Women tend to see all of the obstacles between the goals and where they are—they look at the details.
- Men are sometimes characterized by being insensitive, too tough, a brick for emotions. Women are more sensitive and are sometimes blamed for being too sensitive.
- Men, because they are the protectors and the defenders, tend to be more suspicious. Women tend to be more trusting.

Now God made us different, that He might make us one. Peter wrote in 1 Peter 3:7, "and as being heirs together of the grace of life." In other words, together, we inherit the blessing.

As a husband, I don't believe you can inherit this blessing without your wife. And, she can't inherit this blessing without her husband. God wants us to inherit the blessings together—as husbands and wives.

Now that we have discussed the divine design and the definite differences, let's look at some dynamic directions. We will move from the Old Testament book of Genesis and see how the Apostle Paul brought over the Old Testament story into the New Testament. From his teaching, we will learn how to apply God's divine design in Genesis to our lives today.

Our Culture Is a Little Mixed Up These Days

We have a generation of kids today who are very mixed up. They remind me of the rooster who saw a plate of scrambled eggs and said to the hen, "There go our crazy mixed-up kids."

In our culture today, so many people are confused. They don't know whether they are being raised by a feminine man or a masculine woman. There has been a blurring today of the distinction between the sexes. Most of it was brought about by radical feminists. But the radical feminists are but a tribute to the failure of men to be the kind of masculine men that they ought to be.

Truly, we are living in a generation of miniature men, rather than mature masculine men. We are experiencing the failure of men to lead as God created them to lead. Just think about things like the divorce epidemic, homosexuality, sexual abuse, promiscuity, social awkwardness, emotional distress, and suicide. Honestly, I think primarily, we must lay the blame at the feet of the men.

Remember, when Eve failed, God did not primarily blame Eve, God blamed Adam for Eve's failure. And men must assume their responsibility. (See Romans 5:12, 15, 17-19.)

To Lead Well Men Must Accept Responsibility

Now with that in mind, let me give you five things that we men must do to course-correct and lead as God intended us to lead. So often, when we look at Ephesians 5, the women wince and brace themselves for the sermon about submission. However, I must tell you that, rightly interpreted, Ephesians 5 is a much tougher passage on men.

Now let me tell you what you must do if you would be a masculine, not a midget, miniature man. If you want to have mature masculinity, if you would like to be able to demonstrate to your son or daughter what God's original intent is, and what the divine design is, you are going to find it right here.

First, men must assume responsibility. Look at Ephesians 5:22-23, "Wives, submit to your own husbands, as to the Lord. For the husband is head of the wife, as also Christ is head of the church; and He is the Savior of the body."

Sometimes, we call this verse the Bible's *"Chain of Command."* But the chain of command is not the best way to describe these instructions. Instead, I'd like to call it the *"Chain of Responsibility."*

To be the "head" means that you are responsible. It doesn't mean that you exist to have your needs met because you are the head. It means that you exist to meet needs. Now, husbands, we cannot escape that responsibility. We must lead as the responsible party.

Check out the words of Paul in 1 Corinthians 11:3, "But I want you to know that the head of every man is Christ, the head of woman is man, and the head of Christ is God." I believe that one of our biggest problems today is that there are so many men who have not assumed responsibility. They have wanted to have *headship* without *responsibility.*

When your wife is told to be subject to you, that means she is to look to you for leadership. She is to be able to trust you and put her faith in you. It doesn't mean that she is there to be your servant. Instead, she is to have her basic needs met by you.

The fact that she submits to you means that you have the responsibility to take care of her. You are to lead her like Christ leads—as a servant leader. Wives' submission does not mean inferiority. The devil would have us believe this. But it's a lie out of the pit of Hell.

In Philippians 2:5-11, we read about the incredible model of the Lord Jesus:

> Let this mind be in you which was also in Christ Jesus, who, being in the form of God, did not consider it robbery to be equal with God, but made Himself of no reputation, taking the form of a bondservant, and coming in the likeness of men. And being found in appearance as a man, He humbled Himself and became obedient to the point of death, even the death of the

cross. Therefore God also has highly exalted Him and given Him the name which is above every name, that at the name of Jesus every knee should bow, of those in heaven, and of those on earth, and of those under the earth, and that every tongue should confess that Jesus Christ is Lord, to the glory of God the Father.

May I tell you that Philippians tells us that the Lord Jesus made himself of no reputation, took upon him the form of a servant, and became obedient? And the Bible says, "Therefore God also has highly exalted Him."

Jesus took a low way and God exalted Him. The devil took the highway and God has brought him down and will bring him down to the very pit. We are never more like Jesus than when we have a submissive spirit. Conversely, we are never more like the devil than when we have a rebellious spirit. Submission is not inferiority.

First Corinthians 11:3 reminds us, "But I want you to know that the head of every man is Christ, the head of every woman is the man, and the head of Christ is God." If God the Father is the head of Christ the Son, does that mean that Christ the Son is inferior to God the Father? Not at all. God the Father, Son, and Holy Spirit are co-equal and co-eternal. It would be sheer blasphemy and distortion of a basic Christian doctrine to say that there is inferiority in the Godhead. And yet, eternally, the Lord Jesus Christ is in submission to the eternal Father.

The woman is not at all inferior to the man when she is in submission to the man. What Christian submission is, simply and plainly, is one equal voluntarily placing himself or herself under another equal that Jesus Christ may therefore be glorified.

So often, we talk about husband and wife as a partnership, but a partnership is not the best way to describe it. Don't think of the family, with husband and wife as partners. This is because a partnership has no head. Instead, think of a husband and wife as a team. Let's use a football team for this illustration.

A football team has a quarterback. On a football team, the quarterback directs the plays and the players. Also, the quarterback is the one to call the plays. He does this at the direction of the coach. Does that mean that the quarterback is the best athlete on the team? Not necessarily so. There may be other people on the team who could run faster than the quarterback, have more agility, more natural ability than the quarterback, but the quarterback calls the plays. Why? Because the coach tells him to. And, he follows the coach.

Similarly, marriage works as a football team. God is the coach, the husband is the quarterback, and the wife and kids are the teammates.

Does this mean that the husband is superior to the wife? No, he's just simply the quarterback of the team because the coach says so. That's all. Because the coach says so. It's teamwork. And it doesn't mean that he is more competent than his wife.

Quite frankly, my Joyce is more competent than I am in a lot of areas of life. I'll just have to admit it. Now, I can do some things she can't do. But she is, in some areas, much more competent than I am. Joyce takes care of details in our home that would be difficult for me to take care of. I suppose I could do it, but I am so grateful that she is well-versed in these things. However, God, the coach, has still said that I am to call the plays.

Now when I would call a play in football, many times, there would be some discussion and interaction. One player would come to the huddle and say, "I can move this fellow out of the way."

A wide receiver might say, "I can put a move on that guy, I am free. Give the ball to me, I am free."

Or somebody else would say, "I believe we can, if it's only three yards, we can go right up the middle."

As the quarterback, I would have to listen to all of that. I'd also have to listen to the coach, who may send in a play. Leading the team, I'd take the other players' and the coaches' wishes and advice into consideration each time I called a play. We needed to work together to win the game.

When we're talking about assuming responsibility, the husband may delegate authority but not responsibility. The wife may be the one to primarily take care of finances in your home. She may keep up with and pay all of the bills, balance the budgets, and file the taxes. However, while she has the authority, she does not bear the responsibility.

As men, there's no way that you and I can escape the responsibility. Therefore, if it all works out well, she is to be praised. But if it doesn't work out well, we are to be blamed. Do you understand that? You see, I can delegate the authority, but I cannot escape my responsibility. I am to lead so well that my family will want to follow my lead.

Did you know that the Lord Jesus Christ does not demand His headship? Did you know that the Lord Jesus Christ does not force His Lordship on you? He doesn't do it. If He forced His Lordship on us, we'd all be a little better than we are in some ways, but we would be regimented and mechanical.

We're to love our wives as Christ loved the Church. And we don't demand headship; respect and trust are earned. The Lord Jesus Christ has earned my respect and He's earned my trust. I want to earn the respect and trust of my wife and children as well.

If you are a husband, and you are having difficulty assuming headship in your home, don't try to get them to trust you. Instead, seek to be a person that they will respect. Let your wife learn to respect you as a man of God. As she begins to respect you, she will come to trust you as well. We, as husbands, have to assume responsibility.

To Lead Well Men Must Deeply Love Their Wives

As a husband, you must let your wife know that she is number one in your life. Ephesians 5:25 tells us, "Husbands, love your wives, just as Christ also loved the church, and gave Himself for her," some translations say, "and gave Himself up."

Your wife must know that she comes before the children. She comes before your own mother and father. "For this reason a man shall leave his father and mother and be joined to his wife" (Mark 10:7).

My wife, Joyce, knows that she is number one of all human beings. Of the billions of people on this planet, she is number one in my life. And I know beyond the shadow of any doubt that I am number one in Joyce's life. That gives me a sense of security to think that of all the people who ever lived today and have ever lived, there's one person who loves me more than any other person on the face of the Earth. What a feeling that is to my heart, that she loves me that way. Truly, she also needs to know that I love her, that she is number one.

I need to treat her, therefore, as Christ treated the Church. Jesus loved the Church so much that He gave himself for the Church.

Let me meddle just a little bit here. There are some of you who are not guilty of sexual adultery, but you are guilty of emotional adultery. You are sharing things with other women that ought only to be shared with your wife. It seems innocent, but it is not!

Emotional adultery, if left unchecked, can often lead to physical adultery. Even if it never leads to physical adultery, emotional adultery is a crime and a sin against your wife and a sin against God. There is a woman who needs to be number one in your life. Make sure that woman is your wife.

To Lead Well Men Must Protect Their Wives from Emotional Trauma

Let's consider the third trait of men who lead well. **Men who lead well will protect their wives from emotional trauma.** In Ephesians 5:26-27, we read that Jesus gave Himself for the Church, "that He might sanctify and cleanse her with the washing of water by the word, that He might present her to Himself a glorious church, not having spot or wrinkle or any such thing, but that she should be holy and without blemish."

This is how men ought to love their own wives. Included in this love should be the desire to protect her from emotional trauma and damage. Ephesians 5:27 utilizes this phrase, "not having spot, or wrinkle, or any such thing." That word "spot" means trash, refuse, dirt.

It's your job to keep things from being dumped on your wife, trash being dumped on her. You have to be careful that you're not the guy that dumps on her. When you come home in the evening, don't unload on your wife. Of course, she wants to share your hurts. She does want to know where you are hurting so she can come in and weep with you and caress you and care for you.

But you have to be careful with the things that you unload on her. For me, I've learned that the most important time I spend in the day is the first five minutes at the end of the day.

If I go right through the house and go right to my study, or go right through the house and go right to the television, I have failed my wife. When I get home, I need to go right to Joyce. I need to put her in my arms. I need to hold her. I need to tell her that I love her.

It's even better if I call on the phone before I get there and tell her that I am coming and that I can hardly wait to see her. That's so very important. And, it means so much to her and our marriage.

The word "wrinkle" is also used in Ephesians 5:27. It's an interesting word. This word speaks of an internal wound, a trauma. A wrinkle will show itself sometimes on the face. I'm not talking about the normal wrinkles that all of us get. These aren't the laugh lines and the crinkly places around the eyes.

But I'm talking about sometimes the trauma that comes to a woman who has lived with a man who has been a midget man. These are the wrinkles a woman gets when her man has not loved her as he ought. I can sometimes spot these women. You see them when a woman has a tense, taut face. Her face is drawn because of internal traumas. Pain is written on her countenance.

Preacher Robert Burns suggested that at age twenty, a woman has the face that God gave her. At thirty, she has the face made possible by cosmetics. At forty, she has the face that her masseuse and hairdresser have given her. At fifty, she has a face that reflects the way her husband has treated her. From there on she has the face she gave herself.

A husband is to protect his wife from spots and wrinkles. My assignment from God, sir, and your assignment from God, is to make your wife a more radiantly beautiful Christian.

To Lead Well Men Must Make Their Wives Feel Secure

To lead well, men are to assume responsibility. Let your wife know that she is number one. Protect your wife from emotional trauma. Also, you are to make your wife feel secure. **A great husband will work to make his wife feel secure.** In Ephesians 5:29, we read, "For no one ever hated his own flesh, but nourishes and cherishes it...."

The word "nourish" is obvious. It means to get nourishment. When you are hungry, you want to eat. And when you are thirsty, you want to drink. You want your needs met.

As a husband, it is your responsibility to provide for your wife the physical, psychological, emotional, and spiritual nutriment that she needs to grow. You are to nourish her. You are to help her to grow.

Not only are you to nourish her, but you are also to cherish her. The word "cherish" means to warm with body heat. An illustration of this is a hen sitting on her eggs. When a hen is sitting on those eggs, she cannot be moved. You can come along and kind of walk past, and she will peck at you, but she won't move. A snake will come by, and she will peck at that, but she won't move.

She will sit on those eggs until they are hatched. What she is doing is nourishing them with body heat. That's what you are to do. You provide the nourishment so your wife can grow and "hatch." Give her your best, hold her, cherish her, and watch her blossom. You have the power to do amazing things for your wife!

I heard of a woman who got in almost a catatonic state. Nobody could bring her out of it. They took her to the psychiatrist. He couldn't get much response from her. And finally, he had an idea, and he left his desk, walked around, put her in his arms, held her up close to his chest, and gave her a big kiss.

With that, she just sighed and breathed. The light came back into her face and a smile played across the corners of her cheeks.

Then, the psychiatrist turned to her husband and said, "See, that's what she needs every day of the week."

The husband looked at him and answered, "Well, doctor, I can bring her in for six days, but I can't get her here on Thursdays."

To Lead Well Men Need to Take the Initiative

There's one final thing that men must do to lead well. **To be a great husband, you need to take the initiative.** The husband is to take the initiative. I would say, primarily, if the home is wrong, it is because the husband is wrong. The husband takes the initiative.

We are to love our wives how? As Christ loved the Church. Who took the initiative? Jesus took the initiative.

We love because God loved us. "Out of the ivory palaces, into a world of woe, only His great, eternal love made my Savior go."[2]

Jesus is pictured in the Bible as loving us first. In Revelation 3:20, we read, "Behold I stand at the door and knock." It's not us knocking at God's door, but Him knocking at our door that caused us to open the door.

The Bible says in Romans 3:11, "There is none who seeks after God." God seeks after us. He comes for us. Similarly, husbands are to seek after their wives. Men are to be the initiators and women are to be the responders.

For an illustration of these principles, let's look at Song of Solomon. There is something very interesting about how husbands are to love their wives. This again speaks of the music of marriage.

Here is an entire love poem, actually a song. I want you to see how the male lover, who pictures Christ loving His Church, is pictured here. In Song of Solomon 1:8, He speaks, "If you do not know, O fairest among women." Here He's pursuing her with

---

2. Barraclough, Henry. "Ivory Palaces" *Hymnary.org,* hymnary.org/hymn/HHOF1980/page/140.

beautiful language, and you'll never find more beautiful language than this.

Look at Song of Solomon 1:15, "Behold, you are fair, my love! Behold, you are fair! You have dove's eyes."

You may think that you can't talk like this. Well, maybe you need to work at it. I don't think Solomon just did this overnight.

Let's look at another example. In Song of Solomon 4:1, "Behold, you are fair, my love! Behold, you are fair!...Your hair is like a flock of goats, going down from Mount Gilead."

Consider her response in Song of Solomon 5:2, "I sleep, but my heart is awake; it is the voice of my beloved! He knocks, saying, 'Open for me, my sister, my love, my dove, my perfect one; for my head is covered with dew, my locks with the drops of the night.'" In other words, I've been up all night just trying to get to you, sweetheart.

The man continues to knock on the door. And, she tells him that she is already ready for bed. In Song of Solomon 5:3, she says, "I have taken off my robe, how can I put it on again? I have washed my feet, how can I defile them?" Maybe she lived in a house with a dirt floor and she's saying, "Look, I'm already in bed, and don't bother me now." She seems to be pretending she doesn't want to go to the door.

But then we read the next verse. "My beloved put his hand by the hole of the door, and my bowels were moved for him" (KJV). What the word "bowels" means is the innermost being.

If this were in modern language, it would read more like this. The man would say, "Would you open the door, honey? I want to put my arms around you."

Pretending to be hard to get, she says, "Oh, no, I'm already in bed. I've already taken off my clothes and put on my pajamas and I've washed my feet."

But he continues to knock. He wants to get in and see her. He has traveled a long way to see her. This seems to bring her joy and make her heart beat faster. In fact, in verse 5, we read that she is not in the bed. She is putting on perfume. Look at Song of Solomon 5:5, "I arose to open for my beloved, and my hands dripped with myrrh, my fingers with liquid myrrh, on the handles of the lock."

This woman in the Bible loved being pursued by her man. Your wife will love to be pursued by you as well. She wants to be pursued. And, it's the husband who is to take the initiative.

Did you know that if you don't take the initiative in loving your wife that you are going to cause her trauma? If she has to take the initiative, it will hurt her. Something in her very spirit will be wounded because God did not make her to be the one to take the initiative. God gave you, as the husband, this job.

If the woman initiates, she doesn't feel right. Now I'm not talking about a woman flirting with her husband. That is great. Of course, she can. But if the total import of life is the woman taking the initiative, there's something vitally wrong in the marriage.

Notice what Proverbs has to say about this. Remember that husbands are to love their wives as Christ loved the Church. And Christ took the initiative. Do you know what the mark of a harlot is? The mark of a harlot is somebody, a female, who is brazen and who takes the initiative with men.

Look at Proverbs 7:10, "And there a woman met him with the attire of a harlot." The dress of a harlot. Did you know there is the dress of a harlot? Some women go outside in things they ought not to have come downstairs in. The Bible calls it the attire of a harlot.

Some women suggest that they just want to be attractive. You better ask yourself, "What are you trying to attract?"

What is not for sale should not be advertised. Did you know that? The Bible speaks of the attire of a harlot. Yes, a woman ought to dress beautifully. But not with suggestiveness. When women dress suggestively or immodestly, the Bible calls that the attire of a harlot.

The Bible also talks about this woman being loud and stubborn. Ladies, God never made you to be a loudmouth or a mulish person in public. It is not feminine; it is a form of harlotry. In the second part of Proverbs 7:11, we read, "Her feet would not stay at home."

This woman is out in the streets, "...lurking at every corner" (Proverbs 7:12). She's not a keeper at home. She is not under protection. She is out in public on the streets. And notice how she is the aggressor.

> So she caught him and kissed him; with an impudent face she said to him: "I have peace offerings with me; today I have paid my vows. So I came out to meet you, diligently to seek your face, and I have found you. I have spread my bed with tapestry, colored coverings of Egyptian linen. I have perfumed my bed with myrrh, aloes, and cinnamon. Come, let us take our fill of love until morning; let us delight ourselves with love" (Proverbs 7:13-18).

These are all the marks of the harlot. Many fathers have confided in me that their sons now are having difficulty dating girls because so many of the girls say, "If you don't sleep with me, we can't date anymore."

That's almost unthinkable. Now God demands as much purity from a man as he does a woman. But we live in a day today in which the feminist has done such a job on us, that it is now the women who are becoming the aggressors. God never intended that. It isn't His divine design.

Men are the ones who are to initiate. So, what is the issue? Remember previously I told you that men are goal oriented. Often, once men reach the goal of marrying a girl, they are off to pursue another goal. Once they get married, they think the work is done. But, that's just when the woman is getting started. Most women can hardly wait till they get married because they think it's going to be one perpetual courtship. When the man quits pursuing her, she wonders what has happened.

Just the other day Joyce asked me, "Adrian, remember how you used to come in when we were courting and would stand by me in the kitchen? We were at my mother's house, and you would help me to do the dishes?"

I laughed when I thought about the fact that it wasn't the dishes I was after. I was after her. When she had both hands in the sink, I could come up behind her and give her a big hug. Like most young men, I was very goal oriented. I wanted to marry this girl. Honestly, I'd help with the dishes to get to be with her and to get to hug her.

Most men won't run after something they have already caught. It's just how we are made. We have to work at it to continue to initiate, chase, and pursue our wives after we marry them.

I heard about one young woman who was talking with her mother. She said to her mom, "My boyfriend is just spending so much money on me. I don't know what to do about it, Mom."

Her mother flatly replied, "Just get married. He will stop."

Dating and courtship should not end with the marriage ceremony. You need to turn up the heat and keep pursuing your wife.

A Few Final Thoughts

Men, hear what I am saying. God made us different that he might make us one. But God gave you one nature and God gave your wife another nature. And God gave you masculinity and God gave you the responsibility that you are to assume.

You may give your wife authority, but you can never get rid of your responsibility. Be sure to let your wife know that she is number one. And once you let your wife know that she is number one, you move in to protect your wife from those internal traumas. Seek to present her without spot or wrinkle, to make her a more radiantly beautiful Christian.

And then, my dear friend, once you have done that, you move in to encourage her, that is to nourish her and to cherish her. And it is up to you sir to take the initiative. All of us, including this preacher, are going to have to begin to practice what God's Word has said, that there might be harmony in the home.

A Prayer for Our Homes:

Father God, I just pray that You would help us to understand what is important. Lord God that we would not see money as a goal but as a tool, and that we will not sacrifice our families to gain money or time, but that we might sacrifice money, time, or anything else for the goal of a Christian home that glorifies You. In Jesus' Name, Amen.

"I think one of the major obstacles to the 'music of marriage' is tension in the home."

—Adrian Rogers

Chapter Three

WHEN THE STRING SNAPS

For the last two chapters, we've discussed harmony and melody in the home. Husbands and wives are to sing the same song, but they sing different parts. That's what makes it harmonious. We make wonderful harmony when we play the parts that God has equipped us to play.

Next, let's think about some of the challenges that may arise in the home. I want us to think about this subject: *"When the String Snaps."* What do we do when there is tension in the home?

Consider the words of Proverbs 15:13-22:

> A merry heart makes a cheerful countenance, but by sorrow of the heart the spirit is broken. The heart of him who has understanding seeks knowledge, but the mouth of fools feeds on foolishness. All the days of the afflicted are evil, but he who is of a merry heart has a continual feast. Better is a little with the fear of the Lord, than great treasure with trouble. Better is a dinner of herbs where love is, than a fatted calf with hatred. A wrathful man stirs up strife, but he who is slow to anger allays contention. The way of the lazy man is like a hedge of thorns, but the way of the upright is a

highway. A wise son makes a father glad, but a foolish man despises his mother. Folly is joy to him who is destitute of discernment, but a man of understanding walks uprightly. Without counsel, plans go awry, but in the multitude of counselors they are established.

I want you to notice some words in this passage of Scripture:

- sorrow
- afflicted
- trouble
- hatred
- strife

Now all these words are synonyms for strife. I suppose we might also use words like "tension" or "stress" as well. All of these are times when the fiddle string gets too tight.

Lately, I've become quite a musician studying the "music of marriage." As I've studied, I've discovered that when the violin string is not tight enough, the music is flat and dull. But if the string is too tight, the music is shrill and high-pitched. And if the string is even tighter yet, the string will snap.

Honestly, I think one of the major obstacles to the "music of marriage" is tension in the home. Stress is related to raising your voice, it is related to raising your pulse, and it is related to raising your children.

I mean if you've got children, dear friend, you have stress just built in. And look at these words again: sorrow, affliction, trouble, hatred, strife. All of these are stress words. Being in today's home, dear friend, I want to tell you that the string can get mighty tight. And sometimes, it can snap.

There Is a Great Deal of Stress in Home These Days

Did you know that domestic violence is a major problem in America? I'm talking about horrible violence in the home

WHEN THE STRING SNAPS

that happens every fifteen seconds in America. About half of all married couples, according to the research that I did, have times in which they experience violence in the home.

In addition, in one-fourth of all marriages, violence is a common occurrence. Did you know that twenty percent of all murders in America happen inside the family unit? Twenty percent! Spouses commit thirteen percent of these murders.

We used to say when we came home, "It's a jungle out there."

Today, we may need to also say, "It's a jungle in here too."

This stress is not just damaging to our homes. All this stress is impacting our health. Stress is a terrible thing. Stress will do the same thing to you that sand will do to machinery.

I read an interesting study recently about the stress that is on fighter jet pilots who land on the decks of aircraft carriers. Among members of the entire crew on these aircraft carriers, those who had to land planes on the deck had much higher cholesterol levels than the rest of the crew. This higher cholesterol was attributed to the stress of their jobs.

You see, that's stress. Now not all stress is bad. It takes a certain tension to make the violin play at all. You've got to have some stress in life. However, too much stress is dangerous to the home. It's dangerous to our health and our happiness.

So, I want to give you four ways to relieve the stress in your home. These are all actions you can take to put the "music of marriage" back there when the string gets too tight. When you're so stressed out that you don't know what to do, you are going to go to the Word of God. The words of wisdom from the Proverbs are going to offer us wonderful admonitions for our homes and for our hearts.

To Keep the String from Breaking, Learn to Laugh

Now, you may be surprised at this first admonition: learn to laugh. Just learn to laugh. Consider the words of Proverbs 15:13, "A merry heart makes a cheerful countenance."

Have you ever seen people who claim to be saved, but they look like they are always living with gallbladder attacks? If they have merry hearts, the Bible says it's going to show up on their faces. Proverbs 15:13 says, "A merry heart makes a cheerful countenance, but by sorrow of the heart the spirit is broken."

When the Bible says, "the spirit is broken," this means that the string has snapped in a life. The spirit of a person is the wellspring of life. That is the true inner person, that deepest part of our lives. When the spirit is broken, the zest, the enthusiasm, the spark, the thrill, the fight is gone out of life.

On the contrary, having a merry heart is wonderful medicine. A merry heart is the sign of happiness. Happiness and joy are not the same things, but they are related. They are first cousins. Joy is that constant presence of God no matter what happens. To have a merry heart is to capture and enjoy those wonderful times of life.

I've heard it said that "laughter is the mind sneezing." I like this!

Did you know that there are three things that animals don't do that human beings do? There may be more, but there are three I want to mention. Animals don't blush. Humans are the only animals that can blush and the only ones that need to. Also, animals don't cry. No animal weeps. You might think your dog is weeping, but dogs don't cry.

The third thing animals don't do is laugh. They don't blush, they don't weep, and they don't laugh. What this tells us is that since we are made in the image of God, we are to reflect His character. God is a God of joy and laughter. These are gifts from God to us. There is nothing wrong with laughter. It is a special gift from God.

Laughter comes innately. You don't have to teach children to laugh; you have to teach children when not to laugh. And if you have the joy of the Lord in your heart, it's going to show up on your face. Look at Proverbs 15:13 again, "A merry heart makes a cheerful countenance."

What's another word for a cheerful countenance?

Smile. Let me share something about a smile. This was written by an anonymous author, but I think it is incredible.

A smile: It costs nothing but creates much good. It enriches those who receive it without impoverishing those who give it away. It happens in a flash, but the memory of it can last forever. No one is so rich that he can get along without it. No one is too poor to feel rich when receiving it. It creates happiness in the home, fosters goodwill in business, and is the countersign of friends. It is rest to the weary, daylight to the discouraged, sunshine to the sad, and nature's best anecdote for trouble. Yet, it cannot be bought, begged, borrowed, or stolen, for it is something of no earthly good to anyone until it is given away willingly.

I love this! When you dress up in the morning, don't forget to put on a smile. And don't be ashamed of your sense of humor. Your sense of humor is a gift from God. Also, it has been psychologically documented that laughter, along with a well-rounded sense of humor, is one of the surest signs of intelligence. Doesn't that make you want to smile and laugh more?

Now, I'm not talking about unwholesome laughter; I'm not talking about cheap, coarse, degrading humor; the Bible warns against that. The Bible says in Ephesians 5:4 that we are warned against filthiness and foolish talking and jesting which are not fitting. Crude jokes, sexual innuendos, and all of these things have no place in our lives.

But good, wholesome laughter is a gift from God. Abraham Lincoln said that God must have meant for us to laugh, or else "He would not have made so many mules, parrots, monkeys and human beings."

God wants us to laugh.

God gave Sarah a little child, and God told her to name that child "Laughter." We call his name Isaac. The name Isaac means laughter. We read this in Genesis 21:6, "And Sarah said, 'God has made me laugh, and all who hear will laugh with me.'" She was laughing at what God did when He gave that home a little boy that brought such joy that they called his name, Laughter.

Consider another verse on laughter. In Luke 6:21, we read about Jesus as He is looking at people who are downtrodden and sorrowful. Jesus says, "Blessed are you who hunger now, for you shall be filled. Blessed are you who weep now, for you shall laugh." That's what Jesus says: "You shall laugh."

Yes, there's a time to weep; but you had better put some laughter in your home, especially when times get tough. Laughter is one of God's ways to help to break the tension when the string gets too tight.

As I think about the home where I grew up, we were constantly laughing. My home was the most fun place that I knew of. One time, as a great hurricane was about to pass through our West Palm Beach, Florida, neighborhood, my dad was out with others nailing shutters and boarding things up before the storm. The winds were rough, it was already raining, and the power was out.

My dad came into the house; his hair was blown, and he was soaked to the bone. I was a little fellow, watching my dad and wondering really how serious the situation was. As my dad entered the kitchen, he seemed weary, and his shoulders were drooping a little. You could tell he was tired.

He looked at my mom and said, "I'd give five dollars for a cup of coffee."

The electricity was off, but my mama just opened the kettle and put some water in and turned on the stove. The gas wasn't off. I guess my dad had forgotten that. With ease, my mama made him a quick cup of instant coffee.

Then, I watched my dad reach in his pocket and pull out five dollars and give it to my mama. Then, they both began to laugh. I mean right in the middle of the storm. They sat down and drank coffee, laughing. Somehow at that moment, they made a hurricane not seem important at all. Just that simple act of humor took the tension out of the situation.

As a little boy, I watched them laugh in the face of the storm. It calmed my heart as I observed their humor and saw them find humor amid the chaos. You see, a good laugh is just sunshine in the home.

In my opinion, there are three things you ought to give to your children: life, love, and laughter. If I can give you three simple rules for raising kids, they would be: be fair, be firm, and be fun. That just about sums it up—just be fair, be firm, be fun. These things will help to take the tension out of this awful, awful world that we live in today.

To Keep the String from Breaking, Cultivate Contentment

Not only do we need to learn to laugh, but we also need to cultivate contentment. In Proverbs 15:16-17, we read, "Better is a little with the fear of the LORD, than great treasure with trouble. Better is a dinner of herbs where love is, than a fatted calf with hatred."

What is this talking about? Our Lord is just telling us that so many of us are uptight because our value systems are wrong. We always think we have to have more and more and more stuff. We need a bigger and better house, gourmet food, new cars, amazing vacations, and all of the latest gadgets. However, these things are not going to bring happiness. And often, striving for these things is what brings tension into the home.

Let me give you two scenes that have been pictured in the Bible and see if I can update them a little bit.

First of all, we have a young couple living in a small apartment. The husband comes home to find the wife fixing the meal. They sit down to eat around the kitchen table. No linen tablecloth covers the table. Instead, it is plastic. The dishes don't necessarily match; some of them are even chipped.

At this first home, there is no silver; the utensils are stainless, and some of the forks are bent a little. The furniture is worn. As the children come and sit around the table, the mom serves them all vegetable plates. The Bible calls this a dinner of herbs.

The family gathers around the table and enjoys a meal together. Before they eat, they all take hands and pray over their meal. Truly, they are thankful for God's goodness to them. Then, they laugh, they joke, and they have a wonderful time of fellowship around the table. There in that little apartment, they are blessed.

Then, the Bible details a second scene. In this scenario, we see a big house, a mansion. There are large columns out front and expensive cars parked in the circle driveway. As you enter the house, marble floors greet you, along with incredible decorations, expensive artwork, and a huge dinner table.

As you prepare to be seated, you see an array of delectable appetizers all set out amongst fine china, crystal, and silver. The woman of the house is cold and snooty. The man sits silently as he recovers from his workday. And the children are surly and rude. No one talks. No one blesses the food. No one is grateful.

Instead, the staff serves a gourmet meal prepared by the personal chef. The family scarfs down the wonderful food with very little interaction. When there is talk, it's sarcastic, cutting, and unkind. If there are guests present, there will be some measured politeness.

As you consider both of these settings, which home would you rather be in?

Friend, I would choose that little apartment ten times over! I mean that with all of my heart. A big home without love can be a curse.

I'm not saying that you can't be rich and have love. I've been to many beautiful homes that are also quite loving. If that is your experience, I'm so happy for you. It's a gift of God, and enjoy it. God gives us richly all things to enjoy.

I'm not against you having nice things, but I'm just saying, dear friend, you'd better get your values straightened. You'd better find out what matters. Understand what the Bible says in Proverbs 15:16, "Better is a little with the fear of the LORD, than great treasure with trouble." In other words, better is a vegetable plate where love is than filet mignon where there is no love.

Get your value system straightened out. Beware of the tyranny of things. In 1 Timothy 6:6-8, we read, "Now godliness with contentment is great gain. For we brought nothing into this world, and it is certain we can carry nothing out. And having food and clothing, with these we shall be content."

In 1 Timothy 6:9, we read about "those who desire to be rich fall...." This doesn't say they are rich, but they have set their hearts on being rich. They want to be rich. Have you ever been like this? Do you struggle with wanting to be wealthy?

If your heart is set on being rich above all else, you are in great danger. The Bible teaches us that "...those who desire to be rich fall into temptation and a snare, and into many foolish and harmful lusts which drown men in destruction and perdition. For the love of money is a root of all kinds of evil, for which some have strayed from the faith in their greediness, and pierced themselves through with many sorrows" (1 Timothy 6:9-10).

The Bible doesn't say money is the root of all evil; it is the love of money that is the root of all evil.

Often at graduations, commencement speakers will tell students to try to make all of the money they can make. They always throw in the phrase, "Just make it honestly."

That's the worst advice I've ever heard. If you're trying to make all the money you can, then you're going to be making money when you ought to be doing something else. You're going to be making money when you ought to be praying or going to church or spending time with your kids. If making money is your consuming goal, you are going to miss so many of the best things in life.

No man or woman should have a goal to make all the money he or she can. Yes, we must provide for our families. But, dear friend, when you determine that you're going to be rich, at that moment, you put yourself in a very vulnerable position.

However, when it's our goal to cultivate contentment, we find great joy and great pleasure in our lives.

Look at Proverbs 15:27. In this verse, we are told, "He who is greedy for gain troubles his own house." When I counsel young people, I often tell them something about money. Here's what I will say: "It's far better to marry a person who's worth millions in character that doesn't have a cent than to marry a person who has a million but is not worth a cent."

To find out what the character of that person is, see if that person loves God. Listen: godliness with contentment is great gain.

Epicurus, the philosopher, once said, "to whom little is not enough, nothing is enough."

Having food and clothing, learn to be content. That doesn't mean that you can't try for more and it doesn't mean that God doesn't want you to prosper. The Bible says that God takes pleasure in the prosperity of His servants.

But you learn to be content with whatever you have and praise God. If you don't, I can tell you, before long, the string is going to snap. And that big house won't mean anything to you, not a single thing.

To Keep the String from Breaking, Alleviate Anger

To relieve stress in our homes, we must learn to laugh and cultivate contentment. **Another way to keep the string from breaking is to alleviate anger.** Alleviate anger. Look again at Proverbs 15:18. The Bible says, "A wrathful man stirs up strife, but he who is slow to anger allays contention." Another word for strife is "stress."

Not all anger is bad. Jesus was angry, but he was angry at the right things. The Bible says in Ephesians 4:26, "Be angry, and do not sin." Additionally, in Proverbs 14:17, the Bible says, "A quick-tempered man acts foolishly." We read in Proverbs 18:13, "He who answers a matter before he hears it, it is folly and shame to him."

Proverbs 29:20 tells us, "Do you see a man hasty in his words? There is more hope for a fool than for him." Be slow to anger, and listen, the way to control your anger is to control your words. And, then in Proverbs 15:1, we read, "A soft answer turns away wrath, but a harsh word stirs up anger."

In my own life, I have to watch what I say. Often, one word just builds the next word and that builds the next word, and it gets worse and worse. Learn to control your speech. The Bible says to be "slow to anger." (See Proverbs 15:18.) You may think you can't control it. You're a liar. You can control it. Yes, you can.

As I was speaking to a group of men the other day, I was talking about this. It's so easy to get home from work and start snarling and fighting and snapping and getting down one another's throats. How quickly we can allow our voices to be full of hostility.

And then the phones will ring. Right in the middle of arguments, people will call. When we answer, we don't snarl at the callers. Instead, we put on our nicest voices and talk to the people on the other ends of the lines. Have you ever been guilty of this?

We can control our anger. You and I had better learn to control it because if we don't control it, we're going to get out of control. Learn to alleviate anger and watch what you say.

I heard about a man pushing a child in a stroller. As he walked, he said, "Easy, Harold. Easy, Harold. That's a boy, Harold. You're doing fine, Harold."

And somebody said, "It's just so wonderful the way you're so patient with little Harold."

The man answered, "Oh, no. The baby is Albert. My name is Harold."

To Keep the String from Breaking, Walk in Wisdom

There's one more suggestion that I have for you to keep the string from breaking. Not only, dear friend, must you learn to laugh, cultivate contentment, and alleviate anger. **But lastly, you must walk in wisdom.** Walk in wisdom.

Look at Proverbs 15:21-22, "Folly is joy to him who is destitute of discernment, but a man of understanding walks uprightly. Without counsel, plans go awry, but in the multitude of counselors they are established."

Now, friend, if you bring the wisdom of God into your home, you will calm the stress. The stress in your home is simply a sign that you have forsaken the wisdom of God. God is not the author of confusion. God gives wisdom.

For the family to have wisdom, it must come together in a family council. Notice Proverbs 15:22, "in the multitude of counselors" this wisdom is established. You need, as a family, to come together. As I look back on my family life, I wish my family had done more of this.

We had family worship, but I wish we had spent more time in the family council. I wish I had spent more time bringing my children together to let them know what was happening in our family.

We did have some family council time. The children would talk about what was happening in their lives. We would make decisions together, talk about responsibilities, and even make a family budget. In these family meetings, we would talk about allowances, issues, rules, discipline, and whatever else we needed to discuss. As the leader of our home, I would lead these family council times, but I would also really try to listen to hear the hearts of my wife and children.

If you want to take the strife out of your home, bring those children together, sit down together, and talk about everything.

A Few Final Thoughts

As we close this chapter, I want to share one more thing. I believe we often think that we have strife because we have so many problems. But everybody has problems. Every family has issues.

However, families that deal with problems the right way, learn to attack the problems and not one another, can succeed. Sit down and walk in wisdom. Try to understand the other people. Try to see it from their viewpoints. Listen to your children's viewpoints. Try to sit where the children sit. See it through their eyes. Empathize. Sympathize. Understand.

Sometimes a young paperboy is a better psychologist than a husband. Sometimes a husband will come home, and his wife will snap at him and growl at him. Then, he will pick up a verbal club and answer back in anger. In contrast, the paperboy, who meets a snapping, angry dog on his paper route, learns how not to make an enemy out of the growling dog.

As the paperboy encounters the angry dog, he chooses to be kind to the dog. He could throw a stick at the dog. But, instead, he calls the dog over and starts to rub his head and tries to make a friend. Before long, that angry dog is wagging his tail. The boy showed love and calmed the situation.

When you come home and your spouse is snapping and growling, maybe he or she just needs affection. Maybe he or she has had a horrible day. What if you offered understanding and kindness instead of anger?

If you are the one who has had a horrible day, talk to your family about it. Don't be rude. Sit down at the family council and talk it out. Just talk it out. Attack the problem, not one another.

And when you come to these places where there's a multitude of counselors and there's a difference of opinion, as much as possible, give everybody in the family a chance to save face. You can disagree without being disagreeable. But do it all in the spirit of unconditional togetherness.

Proverbs 15 reminds us to learn to laugh. Cultivate contentment. Alleviate anger. Walk in wisdom. If you don't do these things, then the string is going to snap, and the music will be over.

A Prayer for Our Homes:

Father, thank You for Your Word that's so precious. Lord, I pray that You'll put the music back in our marriages, the melody back in our homes, and the wisdom back in our walks. In Jesus' Name, Amen.

"Dads, if there's going to be the music of marriage in your home, you're going to have to see that God made you the leader of the band."

—*Adrian Rogers*

Chapter Four

FATHER, THE LEADER OF THE BAND

T he Bible places a premium on fatherhood. This chapter is all
about fathers. If there is to be music in the home, the father
must be a good leader. Indeed, he must be the leader of the band.
Let's consider what Psalm 128:1-6 has to say about fatherhood:

> Blessed is every one who fears the LORD, who walks
> in His ways. When you eat the labor of your hands,
> you shall be happy, and it shall be well with you. Your
> wife shall be like a fruitful vine in the very heart of your
> house, your children like olive plants all around your
> table. Behold, thus shall the man be blessed who fears
> the LORD. The LORD bless you out of Zion, and may
> you see the good of Jerusalem all the days of your life.
> Yes, may you see your children's children. Peace be upon
> Israel!

Men are to lead out in their homes. This is not an easy task.
It is difficult to be a good man. It's even more difficult to be a

good husband. May I tell you that this Psalm tells you how you can be a good and happy dad?

Notice how it begins. The Psalm starts with the word "blessed." Do you see that? The word "blessed" in the Hebrew language is in the plural form. Our best translation would be to use the word "happy." And it's a double word. The Psalmist is talking about having double joy. Double blessing. Double happiness. God's plan is for men to be "happy, happy."

However, if men do not follow the instructions in this Psalm, they will be doubly sad, and doubly troubled.

If you'd like to double your joy, then you will want to seek to be the kind of dad that the Bible says that you ought to be and need to be. I want to share five ways that you can be a great dad. These are truths from the Word of God, and they are the standard for us to follow.

To Lead the Band, Dads Must Have Character

First of all, I want you to see the character that men must live. Psalm 128:1 tells us, "Blessed is every one who fears the LORD, who walks in His ways." The prime requisite for being a good daddy is to fear God. To fear God is to be truly happy. It's not exactly how we think the formula might start, is it?

If you were to interview your friends and family members, where might they say happiness comes from? Marriage? Money? Fame? Success? Being physically fit? Having lots of beautiful things?

The Bible says that true happiness and true blessing comes from fearing the LORD. This doesn't mean that we are afraid of God or scared of His ways. The fear of God is pure and clean. To fear God is simply to love God and surrender our lives to Him. It is love on our knees. Honestly, the one who loves God the best fears God the most.

Awesome dads are those who have the kind of character that fears God. As a result of this fear of God, these dads will walk in God's ways and live for God. Men who fear God live differently. They walk in great freedom and integrity.

Are you getting this, dads? There is nothing more important than your integrity and your honor. You may fail in a lot of ways as a dad, but if you will fear God, you will impact your kids. They will see something about your life and want what you have. As they see that you are for real and your God is for real, they will trust you and follow you.

It's pretty simple. You cannot teach what you do not know. And you cannot come from where you've not been. You cannot give what you do not have. You must fear God. You must walk in integrity.

What do you want to be remembered for?

As I was writing this chapter, I was thinking, *What will my children remember me for?* My first thought was that they would remember my sermons. Then, I laughed. I can't even remember all of my sermons. My children won't either.

Then I thought, *What else will my children remember me for? Some office that I was elected to? Or the churches that I have pastored?* Nope. Instead, I know what my children will remember me for. At least I believe it is so. They will remember me for my character. And so will your kids.

This is my prayer: that my children will remember a dad who feared God, followed God, and walked in His ways. That's what I want to leave as my legacy. Don't you?

When our first son was born, Joyce and I were in college. I was working my way through school, and we were living from hand to mouth. It was God's hand to our mouths. At times, it was so difficult. Through eight years of higher education, we worked, and God provided.

During those years, God sent us five precious children. One of our boys is in Heaven. God also gave us two precious daughters and two amazing sons. And they always seemed to want to come in the middle of the night. Our oldest son is Steve, and I remember the night he was born. I was sound asleep when Joyce gave me that elbow. She said, "Adrian, I think it's time."

At that moment, I was scared to death. My heart went BOOM, BOOM, BOOM. Joyce calmly said, "Adrian, you're supposed to call the doctor and tell him that we're on our way."

We lived in a little trailer and didn't own a phone. We didn't even have our bathroom in that little trailer; we used a community bathroom. As I ran out to use the community phone, it was about two in the morning. Everything was locked up.

So I ran to my car to get a tire iron so I could pry open a window to get in and make the call. I knew I could get into trouble, but that baby was coming. I dove through the window, banged up my shins, and fell to the floor. Then, I got up and ran to the phone. It was a payphone, and I had no money with me.

Quickly, I ran back to the house and got a nickel so I could make the call to the doctor. When I finally reached him, he told me he'd see us at the hospital.

Once we arrived at the hospital, they took Joyce back for what seemed like hours. This was in the days before men went back to delivery with their wives. I just paced the waiting room by myself, eager to hear news about Joyce and the baby. After a while, they came out and told me I had a son. Then, they wheeled both of them past me in that hospital corridor. It amazed me to watch my flesh and blood pass by in a little bundle with my wife.

As I went back home to sleep for a few hours, I got on my knees and prayed like this. I said, *"Lord, if I never preach a good sermon, if I never pastor a significant church, if I never have any possessions, that's not the important thing. Oh God, I pray that this boy will know that his daddy loves Jesus. I want my children to think that Abraham Lincoln and George Washington were the Jesse James boys compared to their daddy. I want them to believe in the God that I fear."*

I'm so grateful that I can share with you that all of my children know and love the Lord. There is no greater joy than to hear that my children walk in the truth.

I want to tell you something, Dad. To be a good dad is to be a man with integrity.

You can have lots of other faults, and you likely do. But wouldn't you love for your kids to be able to stand up and say, "Yes, my dad makes mistakes and is not perfect. But I'll tell you what I appreciate about him: my dad is real. He is honest and genuine. And he loves God"?

Your children need a dad who fears God, a dad who walks with integrity.

To Lead the Band, Dads Must Learn Contentment

To lead the band, dads must not only be men with good character, but they must learn contentment in their lives. Notice Psalm 128:2, "When you eat the labor of your hands, you shall be happy, and it shall be well with you."

Do you see the words "happy" and "well"? The Psalmist is speaking of contentment. He's talking here about a working man who goes out and labors. And no matter what his labor may be, whether he works from the neck up, or the neck down, he is a laboring man. When he comes home from work, he eats the fruit of his labor. Truly, there's something very wonderful about honest work. There's something very wonderful about providing for your family and coming home and enjoying what God has given.

God has a way of taking care of the godly. In Psalm 37:25, David testifies, "I have been young, and now am old; yet I have not seen the righteous forsaken, nor his descendants begging bread." In Philippians 4:19, the Apostle Paul echoes, "And my God shall supply all your need according to His riches in glory by Christ Jesus."

Does this mean that God will send you all that you want and desire? No. God is not in the business of meeting carnal desires, but He will meet your needs. In 1 Timothy 6:6, we read, "Now godliness with contentment is great gain."

Do you know what the problem is with many dads? They are simply not content. There is never enough.

A man makes $50,000 a year, and he wants $75,000. Then, he makes $75,000 and wants $100,000. After getting to $100,000, he wants $150,000. And, on it goes. He is never satisfied to just simply come home and be happy with his family. This man is always earning a living and forgetting to live and enjoy his life.

I know a story of a family who wanted to move. The father was one of those guys whose mind was focused everywhere except on his family. As he left for work that morning, his wife said, "Now, honey. Don't forget. When you come back home tonight, the moving van will have come and packed us up. We will not be in this house any longer; we are moving across town today. Don't forget."

He said, "Well, who do you think I am? Do you think I'd forget we're moving today?"

She said, "I do know you. You're going to forget."

He said, "Forget it. I'm going, don't worry about me. I'm not going to forget that we've moved. How stupid do you think that I could be?"

Well, he went to work. Then, that evening, he drove home to the old address. The door was closed, the drapes were gone, and the yard was cluttered with papers. The moving van had been there. He said, "Oh, no, I forgot. How can I face her? And worst of all, I don't even know where we have moved."

So he saw a little boy out there riding on a bicycle. He said, "Son, come here."

As the little boy approached, he asked, "Son, do you remember the folks who used to live in that house?"

The little boy answered, "Yes, sir."

The man asked, "Do you know where they have moved?"

The boy answered, "Oh, Daddy. Mama said you'd forget where we'd moved."

Now, that may seem a little extreme, but some dads are almost that bad. They are never satisfied, and they are always working to meet the next level or the next promotion. Instead of paying attention and enjoying what they already have, they are striving for more.

When I look back on my own family life, we had our share of heartaches.

Chief among those was losing one of our children in a crib death. He died of sudden infant death syndrome. Right before that little boy died, we had just moved to our first church out of seminary and bought a few hundred dollars' worth of furniture.

You would hardly call it furniture. We were going to school and were only able to purchase a little couch and a little coffee table. And I was grateful for it.

When our baby died, I remember coming back to that little house and looking at that furniture. I thought, *How absolutely, abjectly worthless is that junk compared to my baby boy.*

At that time, I saw how worthless the things of this world are in comparison to the things that count. Yes. I like having nice things. I want nice things, and I hope you have nice things.

But Joyce and I made up our minds then and made a vow that we would never get upset over the loss of anything material. It's never been our desire to own anything. We may have the title to it, but we are only stewards. Dear friend, this decision has been very freeing for us.

To be a great dad, I want to challenge you to learn to be content.

To Lead the Band, Dad Must Love Mom

A third way for men to lead the band is to deeply love their wives. Look in Psalm 128:3, "Your wife shall be like a fruitful vine in the very heart of your house."

What does a vine do? A vine grows up a wall or a fence. And if it's fruitful, it breaks out in clusters of grapes. God describes the wife this way, as a fruitful vine. That means, she is a faithful wife, because she clings to him, just like a vine clings to a wall. He is her support.

A husband is to be to a wife what a wall or fence is to a vine. He is to be the support. He is to be the strength. He is to have that rock-like strength. And she is to have that tenderness. The wife is to put out her tendrils, and she is to cling to him alone. She is to be a faithful wife and she is to be a fruitful wife.

Does that characterize your wife? By the way, the next time you criticize your wife's judgment, remember she married you!

This verse also mentions children. In Psalm 127:3, we read, "Behold, children are a heritage from the LORD. The fruit of the womb is a reward." Then, in Psalm 128:3, we read, "Your wife shall be like a fruitful vine." These two Psalms are put side by side on purpose. Both are about the home.

From these two Psalms, we learn: children are not a burden; children are a blessing. However, more and more in our society, couples are choosing not to have children. They'd rather have a nicer house and better cars. As they read about how much it costs to raise children and put children through college, they decide not to have many children.

Having children is expensive. We certainly knew what it was like to suffer from *"mal-tuition."*

But let me tell you something. The Bible says that children are a heritage of the LORD. Your wealth is not your heritage. Your house is not your heritage. None of your possessions are your heritage.

Some will say, "Children make a rich man poor."

I would argue, "Children make a poor man rich."

You can't take your money to Heaven. But you can take your children. I'm taking all of mine. How about you? Are you taking your children with you to Heaven? Truly, children are the heritage of the LORD.

Faithful fathers lead by having integrity and good character, by being content, by loving their wives, and by leading their children.

To Lead the Band, Dad Must Lead the Kids

Another trait of the leader of the band is that he leads his children well. Look again at Psalm 128:3, "Your children like olive plants all around your table." Children like olive plants. That's the goal.

Did you know that the olive is a symbol in the Bible of fruitfulness and righteousness? The Psalmist said in Psalm 52:8, "But I am like a green olive tree in the house of God; I trust in the mercy of God forever and ever." Do you want your children to be like green olive trees in the house of God? Do you want them to trust in the mercy of God?

Here's the idea of this passage. You and your wife are like the olive tree. Around your tree are green olive shoots that are coming up. This olive is just reproducing itself in its children. This is what the Psalmist is talking about.

Did you know that an olive tree, if it's well established, can produce fruit for twenty generations? An olive tree is slow to grow. It's a thing of beauty, a thing of productivity, and a thing of fruitfulness.

Now, let me tell you something, Dad. Your wife is like a vine, your children are like olive plants. What does that mean you must do? Cultivate both! Wise is the dad who understands therefore that it is his duty and privilege to cultivate his wife's love and her needs, and to cultivate his children and their needs.

Do you know what the curse of today is? It's not juvenile delinquency. It is not a generation gap. It's not politics. I'll tell you, my dear friend, what the curse of today is. It is not primarily working mothers; it is not the feminist movement. Often, we men like to shove away the blame onto everyone and everything else.

May I tell you what the curse of our society is today? Dropout dads.

If you are absent, aloof, uninvolved, or uninterested in the lives of your children, can I tell you what will happen to your daughters? If your girl does not have a dad's love, she's going to reject her own attractiveness. She's going to get the idea that she is not pretty. She may even reject her own femininity. If her dad doesn't find her attractive, how could anyone else?

She could also develop an inordinate craving for attention. She's going to love to be held. And she'll never seem to get enough. And it's going to make her vulnerable to some young man who will gladly give her those embraces in exchange for other pleasures.

I'll tell you what else your lack of attention is going to do to your daughter. She is going to be given to a spirit of rejection. And when she sees any kind of hostility, big or small, any kind of inconsistency in somebody else, she's going to believe it's rejection. Because she felt like you rejected her, she'll feel this same emotion in all of her relationships.

Further, if you don't spend time with her and cultivate her, your daughter, she is going to seek the company of older men. She may even marry an older man. Because what she is looking for, somehow, is a dad. She may even marry a "daddy" figure because of what she missed with you.

Saddest of all, if you don't cultivate a relationship with your daughter, she is going to find it difficult to trust her heavenly Father. Because of the poor relationship she has had with you, she will have a hard time loving, knowing, and trusting her heavenly Father.

Dads are so significant in the home!

Let's think about the effect of a dropout dad on a son, an absentee dad on a son. I'll tell you what's going to happen. Your son will put up huge walls and keep people at a distance. Because you didn't pay attention to him and love him, he will have a hard time getting close to anyone else. He'll cover his pain by acting tough. But, deep inside, he will be plagued by insecurity.

Our boys need to know the love of their fathers. Moms cannot fill this void by themselves. Many sons will look for role models. And, if your son doesn't become hardened, he may become a more feminine man. You might be sowing the seeds of homosexual interaction in him. He wants your love, dad. He wants you to hug him and kiss him.

If he doesn't understand that kind of love, he may think that sex is love. That's why so many boys are running around with so many issues. Your son will have the same feelings of rejection that a daughter may have. Sons and daughters desperately need the love, attention, and affection of their fathers.

Do you know what the problem is with so many dads? I'll tell you, very frankly, dear friend: we live in a day in which it's easier to make money than it is to be a daddy. We hire professionals to do for us what we ought to do for ourselves.

For example, it used to be that dad would sit in an easy chair and read stories to the children. You don't need to read books to the children anymore. Just turn on the television or hand them a mobile device. Those things will keep them busy. Right?

Since you don't have to read to the kids anymore, you have more time to work and make money. You can buy a bigger house and a bigger television and more electronic devices.

Also, you don't have to teach your kids anymore. You can send the kids off to school and the professionals will educate them. From eight to three, five days a week, someone else can teach the kids. You'll have more time to make more money.

You won't even have to mow the grass or take care of the lawn. Your children won't have to learn these things either. You can have a professional come over and mow the lawn and take care of the yard. This way, your kids are free to do whatever they want. You'll have time to work more and make more money.

Also, if your kids want to learn a sport, you won't have to go out at dusk and throw or kick the ball with your kids. You can let them join one of those clubs. A professional will teach him how to hold a bat. A professional will teach him how to throw a curve. Some coaches can teach your girl how to shoot a basket or kick a goal. Of course, you can buy them great equipment, because you are making so much money!

In addition, you don't have to teach your kids how to swim. You can hire someone to do that. Just work hard, make a lot of money, and buy a swimming pool. Then, you can pay instructors to teach them to swim.

And when your child gets to high school and has trouble, you're going to have enough money to get him a professional counselor. Only the best for your kids, right?

When it's time for your children to drive, you can hire a professional to do this as well. You'll be able to buy them new cars. This is awesome! Your kids won't have to drive old clunkers and get jobs. You can just give them new cars.

The problem with all of this is simple: our kids don't need professionals to raise them. They need dads. They need you! Better an amateur dad than any professional you can pay. Good dads raise green olive trees around their tables.

THE MUSIC OF MARRIAGE

To Lead the Band, Dad Must Leave a Contribution

There's one last thing I want you to see. Dads not only need to lead their children, but they also need to leave a contribution.

Look in Psalm 128:4-6, "Behold, thus shall the man be blessed who fears the LORD. The LORD bless you out of Zion, and may you see the good of Jerusalem all the days of your life. Yes, may you see your children's children. Peace be upon Israel!"

Oh, what a blessing that would be—your children's children, your grandchildren, serving the Lord. Isn't that what you want?

But you may feel so inadequate. Can I tell you that we all do? That's the reason I'm so glad for Psalm 128.

I'm also thankful that in Psalm 127:1 we read, "Unless the LORD builds the house, they labor in vain who build it."

You see, you can't do it. I can't do it.

God will do it, and He'll do it in and through you.

A Few Final Thoughts

I don't know what kind of family you came from. I don't know what your background is. Maybe you were raised in a home where there was child abuse. Or perhaps you were raised in a home where there was drunkenness. Maybe you were raised in a home where there was greed and selfishness.

It may be that you never had a dad who put his arms around you and told you that he loved you. The deepest need of your heart is for a dad just to hug you and say, "I accept you; you're good. I approve of you."

Even though you may not have had a dad like that, I have good news! You can break the cycle. Someone has to break the cycle!

You can't do anything about your ancestors, but you can certainly do something about your descendants. Maybe you didn't have a great home or upbringing, but you can build one. It's not too late.

One father sent me a list of things he would do if he could do it all over again.

Here's the list:

- I'd love my wife more in front of my children.
- I'd laugh with my children more at our mistakes and our joys.
- I'd listen more, even to the youngest child.
- I'd be more honest about my weaknesses and stop pretending perfection.
- I would pray differently for my children.
- I would do more things with my children.
- I would be more encouraging and bestow more praise.
- I would pay more attention to little deeds and words of love and kindness.
- I would share God more intimately with my family.
- I would use every ordinary thing that happened in every ordinary day to point them to God.

Dads, if there's going to be the music of marriage in your home, you're going to have to see that God made you the leader of the band.

A Prayer for Our Homes:

Father God, I've spoken to my own heart, and Lord I pray that You will bring this message home, not only to me but to us. God, give us better fathers. And we thank You, Lord, that we know that You can give us a fresh start. In Jesus' Name, Amen.

"Do you know what America desperately needs? Some good, old-fashioned homes. I believe you will do more by raising godly children than by almost anything else you might do."

—*Adrian Rogers*

Chapter Five

MOM: THE CONDUCTOR OF THE HOME

As we consider the topic of moms, I want us to look at Proverbs 31. In this chapter, you find the picture of what it means to be a wonderful wife and mom.

This is the ideal woman. But, don't get discouraged. A lot of ladies like to stop reading in Proverbs 30; they don't want to go right into Proverbs 31. These traits seem out of reach, unattainable. While reading today, remember, these are standards to strive for—goals to work toward.

I heard about some cows who were out grazing in a field, and they saw a milk truck go by. On the side of that milk truck, there were large advertisements. The ads suggested that the milk was pasteurized, homogenized, sanitized, and vitamin enriched. One of the cows said to the others, "Well, that makes you feel inadequate. Doesn't it?"

Reading Proverbs 31 might make you feel inadequate as a wife and a mom. But I don't want you to feel that way. Instead, I want you to see it for the wonderful picture that it is. It pictures what could be. And I believe it is better to reach for an ideal and miss it, than to aim for mediocrity and hit it squarely.

Let's read and discuss Proverbs 31:10-31 together.

Who Can Find a Virtuous Woman?

In Proverbs 31:10, we read, "Who can find a virtuous wife? For her worth is far above rubies." Then, from this point on, the writer of Proverbs gives us what we would call today, an acrostic. These twenty-two verses that follow, each one of them begins in order with a letter of the Hebrew alphabet.

The writer has arranged a poem, which is a tribute to a virtuous woman. This poem is a great tribute to every virtuous woman. Every great mom. Every amazing wife. You are going to find out that this lady is the conductor of the band, leading the music of the home and family. From "A" to "Z," if we were to use English letters rather than Hebrew letters, we will learn about this maximum mom.

Newspaper columnist Ann Landers once wrote, "It's high time someone took on the free-swinging feminists who have decided for everyone that the married woman who stays home is a brass-plate dummy, a lazy three-toed sloth or a traitor to her Radcliffe graduating class."

Then she went on to say, "Why has the American woman been made to feel ashamed because she is at home cleaning, washing and ironing, and taking care of her children? This was once considered noble and gratifying work. We're told that the hand that rocks the cradle rules the world."

Further, Landers added, "The nesting instinct is a normal and lovely thing, and most women marry because they want more than anything in the world to be wives, homemakers, and mothers. This is not adolescent hogwash or sloppy sentimentalism, it is real; it is what a woman is all about. There's no special magic about a paid job, a great many women who have left jobs, good jobs, insist that the business world is dull and confining, compared with running a home and raising a family." Finally, she added:

> So much has been written about the educated woman's obligation to society, to do something with her education, that one gets the impression that the college graduate who stays home is copping out. I believe that the reverse is closer to the truth. In my opinion, life's classic cop-out is the women who have advocated their responsibilities to their husbands and children, and society, because they lack the maturity to stay at home and do the job they bargained for. To be a successful housewife and mother demands infinitely more emotional balance and moral fiber than is required to hold down a job. Chauffeur, maid, cook, referee, philosopher, rescue squad, hostess, tutor, and psychiatrist, put them all together and they all spell mother. She must be equal to every crisis imaginable. She must expect the unexpected, the child who falls downstairs and cracks his head open, the flooded basement, the busted oil heater, the minor and major battles among her children, coping with these emergencies is the real challenge. How much easier to wiggle into a girdle and beat it out of the house in the morning. That's what millions of American women are doing, and the kids show it.

God's design is for women to be excellent keepers of the home. They were created for it, and they can excel at it. Truly, it is a noble and respectable job. God idealizes that woman as a mother and a homemaker. With that in mind, let's just take this passage apart verse by verse.

Conductors of the Home Are Worthy

As we talk about mom, the conductor of the home, the first thing I want you to see is her great worth. Look at Proverbs 31:10-12, "Who can find a virtuous wife? For her worth is far above rubies. The heart of her husband safely trusts her; so he will have no lack of gain. She does him good and not evil all the days of her life."

To the men reading this…if you are married to a good and godly woman, you are most blessed. As I was writing these words, I was thinking about my own wife. I can tell you that I do not have words in my vocabulary to express to you how much I value my precious wife.

The real value and worth of a wife are not in her outward charm, though I thank God for outward charm. It's not in the beauty of her face, although I thank God for the beauty of my wife. Her real value is her virtue and her character.

"Who can find a virtuous wife? For her worth is far above rubies" (Proverbs 31:10). God does not compare her with a diamond, which only catches and reflects light. Instead, God compares a great wife to rubies. Rubies are beautiful inside and out. They are stunning through and through. This is also true of a worthy woman and wife.

Consider the words of Proverbs 31:30, "Charm is deceitful and beauty is passing, but a woman who fears the LORD, she shall be praised." Of course, there is nothing wrong with beauty. But let me tell you that virtue far exceeds beauty.

Many men have made the mistake of falling in love with a dimple or a smile and then marrying the whole woman. Outside beauty will fade. Inner beauty will just grow and grow. To have virtue is to have moral strength. The Bible tells us that husbands can trust a wife who has virtue. In Proverbs 31:11, we read, "the heart of her husband safely trusts her."

What does that mean? It means that this woman is going to be wise, she's going to be loyal, and she's going to be prudent.

You can trust her with the bank account; you don't have to worry about foolish expenditures and selfish demands.

An anonymous writer once penned these words, "Theirs was a perfect marriage, but for one feminine flaw, he was fast on the deposit, but she was quicker on the draw."

Now the Bible says here, "The heart of her husband safely trusts her...She does him good and not evil all the days of her life" (Proverbs 31:11-12). In other words, she will do him good. She will treat him well. He can truly trust her. This is her great worth.

Conductors of the Home Do Good Work

Next, let's consider the good works of the virtuous woman. Read Proverbs 31:13-14, "She seeks wool and flax, and willingly works with her hands. She is like the merchant ships, she brings her food from afar."

Her work is not all glamour. She is a chauffeur, maid, cook, referee, philosopher, rescue squad, hostess, tutor, and psychiatrist. Put these all together, and you have an amazing woman. It is work, a lot of work, but it is worth it if the Lord Jesus Christ is in it.

The New American Standard translates Proverbs 31:13 in this way. Not only does this woman do all of these things willingly, but, "she does it in delight." It is her delight to do it because she is doing it as unto the Lord.

Once, I read that Mrs. Billy Graham had a sign that hung above her kitchen sink. It read, "Divine services are held here three times a day."

What a great perspective on dishwashing!

Look back to Proverbs 31:14. Notice that convenience is not this woman's most important factor. The Bible tells us, "She is like the merchant ships, she brings her food from afar." What does this mean? She's a wise shopper, a nutritionist, and she goes the extra mile to get the best and to get a bargain. This woman is not all about junk food and fast food.

I heard about a woman whose husband often complained because he wanted a hot breakfast. She gave him a match and said, "Set your cornflakes on fire."

I don't believe that's the kind of woman being described in Proverbs 31. This woman, this ideal woman, wanted to make all things work well in her home. She was a woman of good work and good works.

Conductors of the Home Worship God

Next, we read about this woman being a person who worships God. She is a woman of godly worship. Notice Proverbs 31:15, "She also rises while it is yet night, and provides food for her household, and a portion for her maidservants."

I used to wonder about this verse because she has some maids who help her in this house. This verse tells us she gets up early to prepare the food. I always thought that the maids were the ones who helped prepare. But the Bible tells us that she's waiting on the maidens.

As I read this in the Amplified Bible, I found something very interesting. This is what the Amplified Bible says, "She rises while it is yet night, and gets through communion with her God, spiritual food for her household."

The truth of this verse is, I believe, that she is getting up to have a quiet time with the Lord. We are told in Proverbs 31:30 that she fears the Lord.

What a gift to be married to a woman who loves the Lord! I cannot tell you the times that I have awakened to find my wife already awake singing hymns to our Lord. Or, I'll find her on her knees studying and preparing her heart for the day. My wife is a woman who loves and honors the Lord. Is yours? It's a great gift!

And I think that's the exact picture that our Lord has in mind here.

Perhaps you ladies are thinking...*If I had maids, I could get more done too.*

Can I tell you something? In Bible days, servants were not a luxury. They were a necessity. Today's woman has great machines and appliances to help with all of the work. Dishwashers, refrigerators, stoves, and so much more are available to most families. All of these amenities allow you to save time.

The conductor of the home, the mom, blesses her entire household when she gets up early to have quiet time with the Lord. Her early moments in Bible study and prayer can impact her (and every member of her family) for good.

Conductors of the Home Have Genuine Wisdom

Now, I want you to notice a fourth thing about the conductor of the home. **A virtuous woman has genuine wisdom.** Genuine wisdom. Notice Proverbs 31:16-17, "She considers a field and buys it; from her profits she plants a vineyard. She girds herself with strength, and strengthens her arms."

This speaks of her wisdom. This was indeed a wise woman. Did you know that she was known for her wise investments? In verse 16, we read, "She considers a field and buys it." This Bible woman dabbled in real estate. She not only took great care of her current home, but she also considered additional properties and financial options.

Perhaps you have a full-time job outside of your home. Balancing home and work can be a great challenge.

Can I ask you a few questions about your job, ladies? Does your work enhance your home? Or, does it take away from it? Does your job give you an independent spirit from your husband? Do you feel like you are in competition with your man? If your job hurts your home and your marriage, you may need to prayerfully consider whether or not you should continue to work full time.

Another facet of a woman's genuine wisdom is her physical wisdom. This lady knows how to take care of her health. The Bible tells us in Proverbs 31:17, "She girds herself with strength, and strengthens her arms." She is into fitness and eats right. She doesn't stop caring about how she looks.

Some women will say, "I'm already married. Why should I have to keep working out?"

To this, I would say, "You'd be wise to keep yourself fit. Your appearance greatly matters to your husband. Try to be beautiful and healthy for him, for your marriage, and for your own health and happiness."

Another reason the Bible tells us this woman is wise is that she finds ways to stretch a dollar and save every penny. She is financially wise and economically savvy. In Proverbs 31:18, we read, "She perceives that her merchandise is good, and her lamp does not go out by night."

This woman is a scholar. What he's talking about here is her genuine wisdom. Then I want you to see something else.

Conductors of the Home Give Generously

Women of virtue are also known for their incredible generosity. They care about others and their needs. Look at Proverbs 31:19-20, "She stretches out her hands to the distaff, and her hand holds the spindle. She extends her hand to the poor, yes, she reaches out her hands to the needy."

This lady, this ideal woman, has some skills. She's a nutritionist, a shopper, an investor, and an economist. Now, we learn that she can work with her hands to make beautiful products and gifts. She takes the things she makes and sells them. Then, she gives the money to a poor neighbor or friend.

This woman reaches out to people in need. She's not just taking care of her own, but she also knows how to minister to people who are hurting. And what an impact that must have made on her children. Her generous welfare—she stretches out her hand to the poor.

Conductors of the Home Have Grand Wardrobes

Next, I want you to notice something else. **This virtuous woman had a grand wardrobe.** (Many of you will really like this point!)

Notice Proverbs 31:21-22, "She is not afraid of snow for her household, for all her household is clothed with scarlet. She makes tapestry for herself; her clothing is fine linen and purple." This woman is elegant and well dressed.

The Bible speaks of her scarlet clothing. Wool is about the only fabric that could be dyed with scarlet. We learn that this woman dressed her children warmly. She's not sending them out half-dressed. They are well taken care of.

But not only is she taking care of her children, but she also takes care of herself. She is fashion conscious. I mean, she looks good when she steps out of the house. She is clothed in beautiful garments. Please notice: the Bible never says that because you're saved that you ought to be plain and look unkempt. No, not at all. The Bible puts a premium on looking your best.

Sometimes a woman will come up to me and say, "Pastor, I'm afraid my husband is running around on me."

Well if he is, God will judge him. But, I often want to remind these ladies that they need to continue to look as good as they possibly can.

Think about it. Most men go to work and see beautiful women all day long, dressed up, made up, and looking good. Then, they come home to find their wives in faded housecoats, with messy hair, without any makeup and wearing different-colored slippers on each foot.

Ladies, can I tell you something? There is never an excuse for a man to have an affair. However, don't let your slovenly appearance and careless attitude push him into the arms of a woman who tries a lot harder than you do. Keep trying to look nice for your husband. It does matter to him. God created him that way.

A wise woman will seek to have the greatest wardrobe she can afford.

Conductors of the Home Are Gifted Wives

Now, don't just notice her grand wardrobe but also notice her gifted wifehood. This woman has a great relationship with her husband. Consider Proverbs 31:23-25, "Her husband is known in the gates, when he sits among the elders of the land. She makes linen garments and sells them, and supplies sashes for the merchants. Strength and honor are her clothing; she shall rejoice in time to come."

To her husband, the wise wife is a helpmeet. She enhances him and makes his life better. The Bible tells us that the husband of the virtuous wife was known in the gates. Being known in the gates in those days would be like being well respected and highly regarded in our day. Her husband is a well-known citizen because of her and her actions.

Because this woman does what she does, this husband can do what he does. She helps him to succeed. She builds him up. She greatly contributes to his success.

I can tell you without equivocation, stutter, or stammer, I know that I am what I am today not only because of God but also because of my precious wife. I know that beyond any shadow of a doubt.

And that's what He's saying here. Her husband is known in the gates. She is a woman who is behind her husband, encouraging her husband. Somebody once said, "Behind every good man there is a good woman and a surprised mother-in-law."

I believe this to be true. A woman can make a man great, or she can tear him to shreds. She can build him up or trample him down. A woman to a man is like the wind to a fire. She can either fan the flame or blow it out. Which will you choose, ladies?

Years ago, I read a story about a man whose business completely cratered. He lost everything. He and his wife had to move out of their beautiful home. They had to declare bankruptcy and sell everything.

One night, as they were sitting in their little apartment, he looked over at her sadly and said, "Well, here we are."

She looked at him, smiled, and said, "No, here WE are."

I like that. Here WE are. Together. Husband and wife, facing the future.

A wise wife will learn to handle her husband well.

Conductors of the Home Are Great Businesswomen

Let's consider another trait of a virtuous woman. **A conductor of the home is also a great businesswoman.** She makes fine linen. She sells it, she delivers girdles unto the merchant. This seamstress woman knows how to make money. Earlier the Bible said that she bought a field, then she planted a vineyard.

Where'd she get the money to buy that field?

Well, she knows how to make things and make things work. She is a very wise, very astute woman. She doesn't do this to compete with her husband but to make things better at home. Her business adds value to the marriage and the family. It does not take away from the home; it lends to the home.

Proverbs 31:25 especially stands out, "Strength and honor are her clothing."

This lady is not just clothed with silk and tapestry, but also with strength and honor. Clothed in this way, we are told, "She shall rejoice in time to come" (Proverbs 31:25).

What does that mean?

When a woman like this walks into a room, you're aware of her presence. She has a calm and gentle spirit. And the bad news does not cause her to run for the hills. Under stress, she can smile at the future. She shall rejoice in time to come. Her great trust in God gives her peace.

Conductors of the Home Use Gracious Words

Not only are wise women great at business, but I want you to notice her gracious words. Look at Proverbs 31:26-27, "She opens her mouth with wisdom, and on her tongue is the law of kindness. She watches over the ways of her household, and does not eat the bread of idleness."

A virtuous woman will have control of her own tongue. She will open her mouth with wisdom. Kindness is on her tongue. This lady will not be screaming at her kids or whining at her husband. Why not? Because she got up early to spend time with the Lord, her heart is at peace, and she can live a well-ordered life.

When you lash out at others, it tells more about you than almost anything else. If you're lashing out, you're a person who is not at peace with yourself. And if you're not at peace with yourself, it's because you're not at peace with God. And if you're not at peace with God, it is because you have not had this quality time, this priority time with Almighty God.

A wise woman is a good conductor of the home because she uses gracious words.

Conductors of the Home Have a Glowing Witness

Lastly, I want you to notice that the virtuous woman has a glowing witness. If you look in Proverbs 31:28-31, you read, "Her children rise up and call her blessed; her husband also, and he praises her: 'Many daughters have done well, but you excel them all.' Charm is deceitful and beauty is passing, but a woman who fears the Lord, she shall be praised. Give her of the fruit of her hands, and let her own works praise her in the gates."

This Proverb concludes by mentioning this lady's glowing witness. She has been a witness to her children, who rise up and show her honor. I don't think there can be any greater reward than this—than to have your children honor your walk with Jesus. The Apostle John said, "I have no greater joy than to hear that my children walk in truth" (3 John 1:4).

This virtuous woman was applauded by her own kids. Could there be any greater reward than this? Kate Wiggin has said, "Most of the good and beautiful things in life come by twos and by threes and by dozens and hundreds. Plenty of roses, stars, sunsets, rainbows, brothers and sisters, aunts and cousins, but there's only one mother in the whole world."[3]

In addition to being honored by her children, this woman is also praised by her husband. Great wives need husbands who will tell them that they are great. If you are a husband of a good wife, you need to give her the paycheck of praise and admiration. You need to tell her over and over and over and over again how much you love her. Tell her how much you thank God for her.

By the way, the way the Bible talks about the wife in this passage may have more to do with her husband than with her. I think this man must be the kind of man who has loved her, prayed for her, and freed her to be the kind of woman that she is.

A good man will make his wife even better!

Not only does the virtuous woman's family praise her, but the community gives witness to her character as well. Look in Proverbs 31:31. "Give her of the fruit of her hands, and let her own works praise her in the gates."

---

3. "Kate Douglas Wiggin." *Good Reads*, goodreads.com/quotes/192085-most-of-all-the-other-beautiful-things-in-life-come.

Do you know what America desperately needs? Some good, old-fashioned homes. I believe you will do more by raising godly children than by almost anything else you might do.

Yes. I'm for community involvement, and I thank God for all of the different clubs and charities. I heard about one woman who was a member of several charitable organizations. She was the second vice president of the Society for the Prevention of Cruelty for Orphan Grandmothers with Athlete's Foot.

Finally, after she died, they put a special note on her tombstone. It read, "Here lies Mary Smith. She was clubbed to death."

Think about it. Here's the bottom line. You want your children, your husband, and your grandchildren to be able to say, "We love you, Mom. Thank you for being an amazing mom and person."

A Few Final Thoughts

My dear friend, we have been sold a bill of goods in the day and age in which we live. But the Bible shows us what matters. This Proverbs 31 woman did all that she did because Jesus enabled her.

She was a beautiful person—although her outward beauty is never mentioned. Because of her virtue, she made a difference in the lives of everyone around her. You can too!

A Prayer for Our Homes:

Father God, I pray that You would raise up women who will seek after You. Lead moms and grandmoms to pray, read the Bible, and fall in love with Jesus. Then, empower them to love their husbands and their children. Give them wisdom, insight, and grace. In Jesus' Name, Amen.

"Sometimes marriage that starts as an ideal becomes an ordeal, and then we are looking for a new deal."

—*Adrian Rogers*

Chapter Six

TUNING UP TIRED MARRIAGES

What we need to do is not to look for something new, but to take something old and keep it fresh and wonderful. Peter Marshall, a great preacher of yesteryear, said:

> Dearly beloved, the marriage relationship, when rightly understood and properly appreciated, is the most delightful as well as the most sacred and solemn of all human relations. It is the clasping of hands; it is the blending of lives; it is the union of hearts that two may walk together up the hill of life to meet the dawn, together bearing life's burdens, discharging its duties, sharing its joys and sorrows. Marriage is more than moonlight and roses, much more than the singing of love songs, and the whispering of vows of undying affection. In our day it is by many lightly regarded, and by many as lightly discarded, but marriage will ever remain in the sight of God an eternal union made possible by the gift of love which God alone can bestow.

I think that's so wonderful; I think that's beautiful, and I think that it is well put, but many do not have the *"music of marriage."*

Many do not have a magnificent marriage. Many do not even have a mediocre marriage. Many have a miserable marriage.

I believe that if the devil can hurt us at home, he can hurt us all over. He can hurt us everywhere. He can hurt us in the church, in the school, in society, in the nation, if he has hurt us at home. Satan levels his biggest artillery at our homes. Isn't that right?

When you feel the artillery of Hell aimed at your home, it doesn't mean that you are doing something wrong. It may mean that you are doing something right and that the devil is trying to stop it.

The Apostle Paul wrote the Scripture that we are about to look at. He's a wonderful, wonderful teacher because he tells us not only what to do, but he explains where we are going to get the power to do what we need to do. Further, he gives us an illustration that we cannot miss to show us exactly what it is that he wants us to do. Paul will show us how to love our husbands and how to love our wives.

With that in mind, let's look at Ephesians 5:22-33.

Wives, submit to your own husbands, as to the Lord. For the husband is head of the wife, as also Christ is head of the church; and He is the Savior of the body. Therefore, just as the church is subject to Christ, so let the wives be to their own husbands in everything.

Husbands, love your wives, just as Christ also loved the church and gave Himself for her, that He might sanctify and cleanse her with the washing of water by the word, that He might present her to Himself a glorious church, not having spot or wrinkle or any such thing, but that she should be holy and without blemish. So husbands ought to love their own wives as their own bodies; he who loves his wife loves himself. For no one ever hated his own flesh, but nourishes and cherishes it, just as the

Lord does the church. For we are members of His body, of His flesh and of His bones. "For this reason a man shall leave his father and mother and be joined to his wife, and the two shall become one flesh." This is a great mystery, but I speak concerning Christ and the church. Nevertheless let each one of you in particular so love his own wife as himself, and let the wife see that she respects her husband.

Men, to Tune Up Your Marriage, You Must Tune Up the Leadership

Alright, are you ready? Gentlemen, let's start with you first. I'll start with me. What am I to do if I would tune up my marriage? Well, I am to be the husband to Joyce that Jesus is to the Church. I am to give to Joyce what Jesus gives to the Church.

What does this look like? **First of all, it means leadership.** If you look in Ephesians 5:23, it says, "For the husband is head of the wife." Do you see that? The husband is the head of the wife. How is he the head? As Christ is head of the Church, so also is the husband the head of the wife. Jesus is Lord. He is the Master, but He is not the dictator.

Did you know Jesus never told me to do anything? He never forces me to do anything for Him. So also, husbands are to lead but not to dictate. They cannot boss their wives around. They are to lead with grace as Jesus does. And, if wives refuse to follow, they will reap repercussions. The home is to be a place of order, and God has set up the order.

Marriage rights are a lot like traffic rights. Think about it. If you come to an intersection, and you have the right of way, don't you think you should stop and look both ways? There's a funny poem about traffic rights that I read:

> Here lies the body of Benjamin May,
> Who died defending the right of way.
> He was right, dead right as he sped along,
> But just as dead as if he were wrong.

Now, my dear friend, we learn from Ephesians that the husband is to lead the wife. You are to lead your wife well.

We talk a lot about the chain of command in the home. It's not so much the chain of command as it is the chain of responsibility. To be the head means that you accept the responsibility. Sir, on your desk, as a husband is a sign which says, "The buck stops here."

I want to tell you, mister, if your home is wrong, it is probably because you are wrong.

The great problem in America is not rebellious women; it is slacker, quitter, wimpy husbands. That's the problem in America.

Too many husbands are weaklings and slackers and quitters and shirkers. Too many men will not say, "As for me and my house, we will serve the Lord."

You owe your wife, my dear friend, leadership. Let's talk a little more about your leadership style.

Men, to Tune Up Your Marriage, You Must Tune Up the Love

If you want to tune up your marriage and lead well, then you must also love well. Look at Ephesians 5:25, "Husbands, love your wives, just as Christ also loved the church and gave Himself for her."

What kind of love is this? We may think Paul is talking about romance, but this is not about romance at all. This love is passionate. Now romance may be included, but he's not talking about it here. The word for love here is not the word for erotic love; it is for sacrificial, self-giving love—passionate love.

You see, Jesus loved the Church enough to die for the Church. You ought to love your wife enough to die for her. You may think you do. Well, I'll tell you one way I can find out: do you live for her?

Don't come around here telling me you'd die for her if you don't live for her. You see, a man willing to die for his wife shows it by the way that he lives for his wife. You don't have to die physically to die to your pride, ambition, ego, and your particular proclivities. You can put your wife first. You can start today.

Do you know what most homes need? They need two funerals and a wedding. The husband dies to himself, and the wife dies to herself, and then they are wed one to another. When the Bible says that you are to love your wife as Christ loved the Church, what it means is, nothing is too precious for you to give up for your wife and your home. Nothing, except your relationship to God.

I hope you agree to that. Nothing is too precious for you to give up, except your relationship with God. And I'm going to tell you something else, most women do not mind being submissive to a husband who loves her enough to die for her and shows it by the way he lives for her. Isn't that true?

How are you to love her? Passionately!

But not only a passionate love, but also a purifying love. Consider Ephesians 5:26-27, "that He might sanctify and cleanse her with the washing of water by the word, that He might present her to Himself a glorious church, not having spot or wrinkle or any such thing, but that she should be holy and without blemish."

Did you know that God expects more holiness out of a man than he does from a woman? Did you know that God expects the man to be more spiritual than he does the woman? He expects the man to be the leader. His love for his wife is not only passionate; it is to be purifying.

Do you know what my chief assignment from God is? It is to make my wife, Joyce, an even more radiantly beautiful Christian. You see, I am to love her as Christ loves the Church. What is Jesus to the Church? He is both a prophet and a priest. A man, in his home, is to be both prophet and priest to his wife.

As Jesus has forgiven the Church, husbands should always forgive their wives and not be bitter against them. As the Lord Jesus sanctifies the Church, the husband should also seek to encourage his wife to take every opportunity to live a pure life. Godly husbands never encourage her in any impurity whatsoever.

Another facet of a man's love for his wife should be his protective love. Look in Ephesians 5:28, "So husbands ought to love their own wives as their own bodies; he who loves his wife loves himself."

Here's the deal. If a man is sick and doesn't take care of his body, he will get sicker. Men love and protect their own bodies. They keep them from danger. This is also the way men are to love their wives—as if they were part of their own bodies. Because that woman is a part of that man, he will take care of her.

I have a question: who is closer...mother and child or mother and father?

One woman was asked if she had to choose between her husband and her son, which she would choose. She said, "I'd choose my son; that husband is not related to me."

That's not true. Your husband is a relation of yours. He is part of you, and you are part of him. Sir, if you hurt your wife, you are hurting yourself. Be good to yourself and love your wife.

In your love, protect your wife. Protect her emotionally. Protect her physically. God has given the husband to protect. Many of you men are letting your wife work when you ought to come alongside her and help her. I'm not talking about outside the home; I'm talking about inside the home.

She's tired, and you're sitting there watching television. She's in the kitchen, and you are lounging in your recliner. Get up and help her! Don't make her do it all by herself!

A little boy was looking at an old photo album that was taken many, many years ago. It was a wedding album. He saw his mama when she was a bride. He asked his dad, "Daddy, is that when mama came to work for us?"

You need to give your wife providing love. Look at Ephesians 5:29, "For no one ever hated his own flesh, but nourishes and cherishes it, just as the Lord does the church."

To cherish is to warm with body heat. It means to nurture, to feed, and to mature. What the Apostle Paul is saying, by divine inspiration, is to see to it that her needs are met. Seek to satisfy her as you would want yourself satisfied and, strangely, you will be satisfied. You see, a man, I tell you, is sick who does not want to care for his own body. A man who is committing suicide does

TUNING UP TIRED MARRIAGES

not care for his own body. And a man is committing matrimonial suicide who does not care for the needs of his wife.

The problem is, gentlemen, we fail to think of our wives as a part of us. I mean we think of them as apart from us. So many men think of their wives as possessions, like cars. But, your wife is a part of you, just like we're a part of the Lord Jesus Christ.

Consider Ephesians 5:30, "For we are members of His body, of His flesh and of His bones." When you hurt, Jesus hurts. He's touched with the feeling of your infirmity. And, in the same way, husbands are to love their wives.

Men, to Tune Up Your Marriage, You Must Tune Up the Loyalty

To make sweet music in our marriages, men must also tune up their loyalty. Look at Ephesians 5:30-31, "For we are members of His body, of His flesh and of His bones. 'For this reason a man shall leave his father and mother and be joined to his wife, and the two shall become one flesh.'"

The word "joined" means to be welded or fused to his wife. The two become one flesh. The word "leave" speaks of the priority of marriage. The word "joined" speaks of the permanence of marriage. "One flesh" speaks of the purpose of marriage. It's all right there. Dear friend, that's God's plan. It is loyalty.

The highest of all human relationships, contrary to popular opinion, is not mother/child, nor is it child/parent, it is husband and wife. I hope you understand that. There is no other human relationship like this. Never is it said, of anyone else, that they are one flesh. And so that speaks of the priority of marriage. And to be joined speaks of the permanence of marriage.

Divorce is never the plan of God. Never the plan of God!

You show me a young married couple that keeps divorce as an option, and I'll show you a home that has a great, great potential for disintegration. Take the word "divorce" and cut it out of your dictionary. Cut it out of your mind. Decide that a divorce is never an option for your marriage.

91

Maybe you feel like you just want to cut your losses and start fresh. You want to start over again. The problem with this kind of thinking is that getting a divorce will not fix everything. Couples that get divorced and couples that don't get divorced have the same kinds of problems. The difference is not in the problems that people have, the difference is in the commitment we make to each other.

Get this truth: It is not your love that sustains your marriage. It is your marriage that sustains your love. Marriage is a commitment. The Bible says you are to be joined. A "no-fault" divorce is an impossibility. What happens so often is that a marriage will have 10% problems, and the couple will let the other 90% go down the drain because of a lack of commitment.

Maybe you think you owe it to yourself to be happy. What do you mean by this? When you were at the marriage altar, you made a vow. You owe it to God to keep your vow. You owe it to your wife; you owe it to your children. The Bible says, "What God has joined together, let not man separate" (Mark 10:9).

Possibly you have already gotten a divorce. Take the broken pieces and give them to God. You can't unscramble eggs, but you can find grace and healing in Jesus.

I'm not trying to make you feel bad or heap more sorrow on your life. Not at all. But I am trying to encourage couples who are still married to try to find a way to work it out by the grace of God. Do all that you can do to work out your problems. Commit to each other. Decide to stay together.

One other note is mentioned here. One flesh speaks of the purpose of marriage. We're not just talking about physically one flesh. If that's all one flesh means to you, just a sexual union, then there's little difference in that than animals cohabiting together. That's not love; that's lust. I don't care how much moonlight and roses there may be.

What is the Lord saying here? What is one flesh? To be one flesh is to be one spiritually, one psychologically, and one physically. The marriage relationship—coming together where there is the blending of lives and the union of bodies—is going to be either the nicest or the nastiest of all human relationships.

Think about your front yard—the sod in the front of your house. It looks great outside. But if somebody gets a shovel and takes part of it and throws it on the living room rug, it's just plain dirt. It all depends on where it is and what it is.

Marriage is honorable and the bed undefiled, but adulterers and whoremongers, God will judge. Before marriage, God is not trying to keep you from sex, God is trying to keep sex *for* you. Every time God says, "Thou shalt not," He's just saying, "Don't hurt yourself."

Each time God says, "Thou shalt," He's saying, "Help yourself to happiness."

The Bible says to flee fornication and don't commit adultery. God is not a prude. God loves you so much, He wants you to have the best.

The Bible teaches premarital chastity, post-marital fidelity, and a man and woman relationship only. That's God's plan. You're not going to improve on it. My dear friend, you're not going to change it. God's not going to bend His rules for you or anybody else.

Here's the bottom line: a husband owes his wife loyalty, loyalty, and more loyalty.

Ladies, to Tune Up Your Marriage, You Must Tune Up the Submission

Next, let's consider the role of the wife in God's plan. **If you want to tune up a tired marriage, you must tune up the submission.** If a wife is to be as the Church is to Christ, she must submit to her husband. Look at Ephesians 5:22, "Wives, submit to your own husbands, as to the Lord."

Now I understand that this kind of thinking is the opposite of the ways of the world. Women think they have the right to live as they wish. But, as Christians, we give up our rights. We are crucified with Christ. We belong to Him; we are not our own. We are bought with a price.

Also, when we refuse God's plans, we hurt ourselves. Look at the feminist movement. Now they have many good arguments.

I mean much of feminism is a rebellion against men who have failed. And I admit that so many men have failed. However, we need to correct the problem and not throw away the Word of God.

What has the wisdom of this world done for us? Are homes better today because of the feminist movement? I'm talking about the unwillingness to assume the God-given place in the home. Are homes better? Of course not.

You see, when a woman fails to submit according to God's plan, she's going to have problems with God. You'll have difficulty with God because you're in rebellion with God. Also, you're going to have difficulty with your husband. You'll never be to your husband what God made you to be, and God made you to be a helpmeet. You are to be his completer, not his competitor.

Additionally, you're going to have difficulty with your children. God only gives authority to those who are under authority. And if you never learn to be under, God will never make you over. You'll never have authority in the home.

Instead, you are building rebellion into the lives of your kids. One day, you will pay dearly for failing to obey the Word of God. Moreover, you're going to have personal difficulty, because you are never going to have your deepest needs truly met.

Submission does not mean that you are inferior. Submission does not mean inferiority any more than I'm inferior to a policeman when he tells me to turn right, and I turn right. He's just simply, in that case, the delegated, appointed authority.

Ladies, to Tune Up Your Marriage, You Must Tune Up the Support

Also ladies, to tune up your marriage, you must tune up the support. You need to give your husband a supporting relationship.

Look at Ephesians 5:30, "For we are members of His body, of His flesh and of His bones." What a wonderful, wonderful relationship Christ and the Church share, the most intimate of all relationships.

There is emotional sharing, there is financial sharing, and there is responsibility sharing. Jesus shares with the Church. Husbands and wives are to share. It's the way God perfectly designed things to operate.

A Few Final Thoughts

God's plan, God's way, is not the way to stultify you. He's not trying to hold you back. Instead, God's way is to give you glorious, glorious liberty.

What does the husband owe to the wife? He owes her love. He owes her, dear friend, leadership, and he owes her loyalty.

What does the wife owe to the husband? A submissive relationship, a supporting relationship, and a sharing relationship. Try it, I promise you on the authority of the Word of God, it will put music in your marriage. And it'll tune up a tired marriage.

A Prayer for Our Homes:

Father God, I pray that You would help us to learn what Your Word says. Lord, I pray that husbands and wives together today would just commit themselves to You and to the relationships You want us to build. In Jesus' Name, Amen.

ADDITIONAL TITLES BY ADRIAN ROGERS, JOYCE ROGERS & LOVE WORTH FINDING MINISTRIES

Published by Innovo Publishing LLC

1. *25 Days of Anticipation: Jesus . . . The Fulfillment of Every Heart's Longing*
2. *A Family Christmas Treasury*
3. *Adrianisms: The Collected Wit and Wisdom of Adrian Rogers*
4. *Believe in Miracles but Trust in Jesus*
5. *Discover Jesus: The Author and Finisher of our Faith*
6. *Foundations for Our Faith: A 3-Volume Bible Study of Romans*
7. *God's Wisdom is Better than Gold*
8. *Good Morning, Lord: Starting Each Day with the Risen Lord (a 365 Day Devotional)*
9. *His Story: God's Purpose and Plans from Genesis to Revelation*
10. *Revelation Study Guide (2 Volumes)*
11. *Standing for Light and Truth: Living with Integrity to Shine God's Light in a World Going Dim*
12. *The Music of Marriage*
13. *The Passion of Christ and the Purpose of Life*
14. *The Power of His Presence*

* by Joyce Rogers *

15. *Therefore, I Hope In Him*
16. *Chosen to be a Minister's Wife*
17. *Behold*